PENGUIN PLAYS

THREE PIECES

Ntozake Shange is the author of
the Broadway hit and best-selling
book *for colored girls who have
considered suicide/when the rain-
bow is enuf* and *nappy edges*, a
book of poetry. She lives in New
York City.

*Thank-you,*
*Fozake Shange '85*

# three pieces*

# ntozake shange

penguin books

\* spell #7

a photograph:
lovers in motion

boogie woogie landscapes

Penguin Books Ltd, Harmondsworth,
Middlesex, England
Penguin Books, 625 Madison Avenue,
New York, New York 10022, U.S.A.
Penguin Books Australia Ltd, Ringwood,
Victoria, Australia
Penguin Books Canada Limited, 2801 John Street,
Markham, Ontario, Canada L3R 1B4
Penguin Books (N.Z.) Ltd, 182–190 Wairau Road,
Auckland 10, New Zealand

First published in the United States of America by
St. Martin's Press 1981
Published in Penguin Books 1982

LIBRARY OF CONGRESS CATALOGING IN PUBLICATION DATA
Shange, Ntozake.
    Three pieces.
    Contents: Spell #7—A photograph—Boogie
woogie landscapes.
    I. Title.
PS3569.H3324T5   1982      812'.54      82-9870
ISBN 0 14 048.170 2          AACR2

Printed in the United States of America by
R. R. Donnelley & Sons Company, Harrisonburg, Virginia
Set in Melior

for the children of the world

# contents

# foreword/

## unrecovered losses/ black theater traditions

as a poet in american theater/ i find most activity that takes place on our stages overwhelmingly shallow/ stilted & imitative. that is probably one of the reasons i insist on calling myself a poet or writer/ rather than a playwright/ i am interested solely in the poetry of a moment/ the emotional & aesthetic impact of a character or a line. for too long now afro-americans in theater have been duped by the same artificial aesthetics that plague our white counterparts/ "the perfect play," as we know it to be/ a truly european framework for european psychology/ cannot function efficiently for those of us from this hemisphere.

furthermore/ with the advent of at least 6 musicals about the lives of black musicians & singers/ (EUBIE, BUBBLING BROWN SUGAR, AIN'T MISBEHAVIN', MAHALIA, etc.)/ the lives of millions of black people who dont sing & dance for a living/ are left unattended to in our theatrical literature. not that the lives of Eubie Blake or Fats Waller are well served in productions lacking any significant book/ but if the lives of our geniuses arent artfully rendered/ & the lives of our regular & precious are ignored/ we have a double loss to reckon with.

if we are drawn for a number of reasons/ to the lives & times of black people who conquered their environments/ or at least their pain with their art, & if these people are mostly musicians & singers & dancers/ then what is a writer to do to draw the most human & revealing moments from lives spent in nonverbal activity. first of all we should reconsider our choices/ we are centering ourselves around these artists for what reasons/ because their lives were richer than ours/ because they did something white people are still having a hard time duplicating/ because they proved something to the world like Jesse Owens did/ like Billie Holiday did. i think/ all the above contributes to the proliferation of musicals abt our musicians/ without forcing us to confront the real implications of the dynamic itself. we are compelled to examine these giants in order to give ourselves what we think they gave the worlds they lived in/ which is an independently created afro-american aesthetic. but we are going abt this process backwards/ by isolating the art forms & assuming a very narrow perspective vis-à-vis our own history.

if Fats Waller & Eubie Blake & Charlie Parker & Savilla Fort & Katherine Dunham moved the world outta their way/ how did they do it/ certainly not by mimicking the weakest area in american art/ the american theater. we must move our theater into the drama of our lives/ which is what the artists we keep resurrecting (or allowing others to resurrect) did in the first place/ the music & dance of our renowned predecessors appeals to us because it directly related to lives of those then living & the lives of the art forms.

in other words/ we are selling ourselves & our legacy quite cheaply/ since we are trying to make our primary statements with somebody else's life/ and somebody else's idea of what theater is. i wd suggest that: we demolish the notion of straight theater for a decade or so, refuse to allow playwrights to work without dancers & musicians. "coon shows" were somebody else's idea. we have integrated the notion that a drama must be words/ with no music & no dance/ cuz that wd take away the seriousness of the event/ cuz we all remember too well/ the chuckles & scoffs at the notion that all niggers cd sing & dance/ & most of us can sing & dance/ & the reason that so many plays written to silence & stasis fail/ is cuz most black people have some music & movement in our lives. we do sing & dance. this is a cultural reality. this is why i find the most inspiring theater among us to be in the realms of music & dance.

i think of my collaboration with David Murray on A PHOTOGRAPH/ & on WHERE THE MISSISSIPPI MEETS THE AMAZON/ & on SPELL #7/ in which music functions as another character. Teddy & his Sizzling Romancers (David Murray, sax.; Anthony Davis, piano; Fred Hopkins, bass; Paul Maddox, drums; Michael Gregory Jackson, guitar, harmonica & vocals) were as important as The Satin Sisters/ though the thirties motif served as a vehicle to introduce the dilemmas of our times. in A PHOTOGRAPH the cello (Abdul Wadud) & synthesizer (Michael Gregory Jackson) solos/ allowed Sean to break into parts of himself that wd have been unavailable had he been unable to "hear." one of the bounties of black culture is our ability to "hear"/ if we were to throw this away in search of less (just language) we wd be damning ourselves. in slave narratives there are numerous references to instruments/ specifically violins, fifes & flutes/ "talking" to the folks. when working with Oliver Lake (sax.) or Baikida Carroll (tr.) in FROM OKRA TO GREENS/ or Jay Hoggard (vibes) in FIVE NOSE RINGS & SOWETO SUITE/ i am terribly aware of a conversation. in the company of Dianne McIntyre/ or Dyane Harvey's work with the Eleo Pomare Dance Company/ one is continually aroused by the immediacy of their movements/ "do this movement like yr life depends on it"/ as McIntyre says.

the fact that we are an interdisciplinary culture/ that we understand more than verbal communication/ lays a weight on afro-american writers that few others are lucky enough to have been born into. we can use with some skill virtually all our physical senses/ as writers committed to bringing the world as we remember it/ imagine it/ & know it to be to the stage/ we must use everything we've got. i suggest that everyone shd cue from Julius Hemphill's wonderful persona, Roi Boye/ who ruminates & dances/ sings & plays a saxophone/ shd cue from Cecil Taylor & Dianne

McIntyre's collaboration on SHADOWS/ shd cue from Joseph Jarman &
Don Moye (of The Art Ensemble of Chicago) who are able to move/ to
speak/ to sing & dance & play a myriad of instruments in EGWU-ANWU.
look at Malinke who is an actor/ look at Amina Myers/ Paula Moss/ Aku
Kadogo/ Michele Shay/ Laurie Carlos/ Ifa Iyaun Baeza & myself in
NEGRESS/ a collective piece which allowed singers, dancers, musicians &
writers to pass through the barriers & do more than 1 thing. dance to
Hemphill or the B.A.G. (Black Artist Group)/ violinist Ramsey Amin lets
his instrument make his body dance & my poems shout. i find that our
contemporaries who are musicians are exhibiting more courage than we as
writers might like to admit.

in the first version of BOOGIE WOOGIE LANDSCAPES i presented
myself with the problem of having my person/ body, voice & language/
address the space as if i were a band/ a dance company & a theater group
all at once. cuz a poet shd do that/ create an emotional environment/ felt
architecture.

to paraphrase Lester Bowie/ on the night of the World Saxophone
Quartet's (David Murray, Julius Hemphill, Hamiett Bluiett & Oliver Lake)
performance at the Public Theater/ "those guys are the greatest comedy
team since the Marx Brothers." in other words/ they are theater. theater
which is an all encompassing moment/ a moment of poetry/ the
opportunity to make something happen. We shd think of George Clinton/
a.k.a. Dr. Funkenstein/ as he sings/ "here's a chance to dance our way out
of our constrictions." as writers we might think more often of the
implications of an Ayler solo/ the meaning of a contraction in anybody's
body. we are responsible for saying how we feel. we "ourselves" are high
art. our world is honesty & primal response.

1/22/79  NYC


although i rarely read reviews of my work/ two comments were
repeated to me by "friends" for some reason/ & now that i am writing abt
my own work/ i am finally finding some use for the appraisals of
strangers. one new york critic had accused me of being too self-conscious
of being a writer/ the other from the midwest had asserted that i waz so
involved with the destruction of the english language/ that my writing
approached verbal gymnastics like unto a reverse minstrel show. in
reality/ there is an element of truth in both ideas/ but the lady who
thought i waz self-conscious of being a writer/ apparently waz never a blk
child who knew that no black people conducted themselves like amos n
andy/ she waz not a blk child who knew that blk children didnt wear tiger
skins n chase lions around trees n then eat pancakes/ she waznt a blk
child who spoke an english that had evolved naturally/ only to hear a

white man's version of blk speech that waz entirely made up & based on no linguistic system besides the language of racism. the man who thought i wrote with intentions of outdoing the white man in the acrobatic distortions of english waz absolutely correct. i cant count the number of times i have viscerally wanted to attack deform n maim the language that i waz taught to hate myself in/ the language that perpetuates the notions that cause pain to every black child as he/she learns to speak of the world & the "self." yes/ being an afro-american writer is something to be self-conscious abt/ & yes/ in order to think n communicate the thoughts n feelings i want to think n communicate/ i haveta fix my tool to my needs/ i have to take it apart to the bone/ so that the malignancies/ fall away/ leaving us space to literally create our own image.

i have not ceased to be amazed when i hear members of an audience whispering to one another in the foyers of theaters/ that they had never imagined they cd feel so much for characters/ even though they were black (or colored/ or niggers, if they don't notice me eavesdropping). on the other hand/ i hear other members of an audience say that there were so many things in the piece that they had felt/ experienced/ but had never found words to express/ even privately/ to themselves. these two phenomena point to the same dilemma/ the straightjacket that the english language slips over the minds of all americans. there are some thoughts that black people just dont have/ according to popular mythology/ so white people never "imagine" we are having them/ & black people "block" vocabularies we perceive to be white folks' ideas.* this will never do. for in addition to the obvious stress of racism n poverty/ afro-american culture/ in attempts to carry on/ to move forward/ has minimized its "emotional" vocabulary to the extent that admitting feelings of rage, defeat, frustration is virtually impossible outside a collective voice. so we can add self-inflicted repression to the cultural causes of our cultural disease of high blood pressure.

in everything i have ever written & everything i hope to write/ i have made use of what Frantz Fanon called "combat breath." although Fanon waz referring to francophone colonies, the schema he draws is sadly familiar:

> there is no occupation of territory, on the one hand, and
> independence of persons on the other. It is the country as a whole, its
> history, its daily pulsation that are contested, disfigured, in the hope
> of final destruction. Under this condition, the individual's breathing
> is an observed, an occupied breathing. It is a combat breathing.†

*Just examine *Drylongso* by John Langston Gwaltney, Random House, 1980.
†Frantz Fanon, *A Dying Colonialism*, Grove Press, 1967.

Fanon goes on to say that "combat breathing" is the living response/ the drive to reconcile the irreconcilable/ the black & white of what we live n where. (unfortunately, this language doesnt allow me to broaden "black" & "white" to figurative terms/ which is criminal since the words are so much larger n richer than our culture allows.) i have lived with this for 31 years/ as my people have lived with cut-off lives n limbs. the three pieces in this collection are the throes of pain n sensation experienced by my characters responding to the involuntary constrictions n amputations of their humanity/ in the context of combat breathing.

each of these pieces was excruciating to write/ for i had to confront/ again & again/ those moments that had left me with little more than fury n homicidal desires. in *spell # 7* i included a prologue of a minstrel show/ which made me cry the first times i danced in it/ for the same reasons i had included it. the minstrel may be "banned" as racist/ but the minstrel is more powerful in his deformities than our alleged rejection of him/ for every night we wd be grandly applauded. immediately thereafter/ we began to unveil the "minstrels," who turned out to be as fun-loving as fay:

> *please/ let me join you/ i come all the way from brooklyn/ to have a good time/ ya dont think i'm high do ya/ cd i please join ya/ i just wanna have a good ol time.*

as contorted as sue-jean:

> *& i lay in the corner laughin/ with my drawers/ twisted round my ankles & my hair standin every which way/ i waz laughin/ knowin i wd have this child/ myself/ & no one wd ever claim him/ cept me/ cuz i was a low-down thing/ layin in sawdust & whiskey stains/ i laughed & had a good time masturbatin in the shadows.*

as angry as the actor who confides:

> *i just want to find out why no one has even been able to sound a gong& all the reporters recite that the gong is ringin/ while we watch all the white people/ immigrants & invaders/ conquistadors & relatives of london debtors from georgia/ kneel & apologize to us/ just for three or four minutes. now/ this is not impossible.*

& after all that/ our true visions & rigors laid bare/ down from the ceiling comes the huge minstrel face/ laughing at all of us for having been so game/ we believed we cd escape his powers/ how naive cd we be/ the magician explains:

xiii

*crackers are born with the right to be alive/*
*i'm making ours up right here in yr face.*

the most frequently overheard comment abt *spell #7* when it first opened
at the public theater/ waz that it waz too intense. the cast & i usedta
laugh. if this one hour n 45 minutes waz too much/ how in the world did
these same people imagine the rest of our lives were/ & wd they ever be
able to handle that/ simply being alive & black & feeling in this strange
deceitful country. which brings me to *boogie woogie landscapes*/ totally
devoted to the emotional topology of a yng woman/ how she got to be the
way she is/ how she sees where she is. here/ again/ in the prologue lies the
combat breath of layla/ but she's no all-american girl/ or is she?

> *the lil black things/ pulled to her & whimpered lil black whys/ 'why*
> *did those white men make red of our house/ why did those white men*
> *want to blacken even the white doors of our house/ why make fire of*
> *our trees/ & our legs/ why make fire/ why laugh at us/ say go home/*
> *arent we home/ arent we home?'*

she waz raised to know nothing but black & white two-dimensional
planes/ which is what racism allots everyone of us unless we fight. she
found solace in jesus & the american way/ though jonestown & american
bandstand lay no claims to her:

> *shall i go to jonestown or the disco? i cd wear red sequins or a burlap*
> *bag. maybe it doesnt matter/ paradise is fulla surprises/ & the floor of*
> *the disco changes colors like special species of vipers . . .*

her lover/ her family/ her friends torment her/ calm her with the little they
have left over from their own struggles to remain sane. everything in
*boogie woogie landscapes* is the voice of layla's unconscious/ her
unspeakable realities/ for no self-respecting afro-american girl wd reveal
so much of herself of her own will/ there is too much anger to handle
assuredly/ too much pain to keep on truckin/ less ya bury it.
    both *spell #7* & *boogie woogie landscapes* have elements of magic or
leaps of faith/ in typical afro-american fashion/ not only will the lord find
a way/ but there *is* a way outta here. this is the litany from the spirituals
to Jimi Hendrix' "there must be some kinda way outta here"/ acceptance
of my combat breath hasnt closed the possibilities of hope to me/ the
soothing actualities of music n sorcery/ but that's why i'm doubly proud
of *a photograph: lovers in motion*/ which has no cures for our "condition"
save those we afford ourselves. the characters michael/ sean/ claire/
nevada/ earl/ are afflicted with the kinds of insecurities & delusions only

available to those who learned themselves thru the traumas of racism. what is fascinating is the multiplicity of individual responses to this kind of oppression. michael displays her anger to her lovers:

> i've kept a lover who waznt all-american/ who didnt believe/ wdnt straighten up/ oh i've loved him in my own men/ sometimes hateful sometimes subtle like high fog & sun/ but who i loved is yr not believin. i loved yr bitterness & hankered after that space in you where you are outta control/ where you cannot touch or you wd kill me/ or somebody else who loved you. i never even saw a picture & i've loved him all my life he is all my insanity & anyone who loves me wd understand.

while nevada finds a nurtured protection from the same phenomenon:

> mama/ will he be handsome & strong/ maybe from memphis/ an old family of freedmen/ one of them reconstruction senators for a great grandfather . . .

their particular distortions interfere with them receiving one another as full persons:

> claire
> no no/ i want nevada to understand that i understand that sean's a niggah/ & that's why he's never gonna be great or whatever you call it/ cuz he's a niggah & niggahs cant be nothin.

> nevada
> see/ earl/ she's totally claimed by her station/ she cant imagine anyone growing thru the prison of poverty to become someone like sean

> claire
> sean aint nothin but a niggah nevada/ i didnt know you liked niggahs.

such is the havoc created in the souls of people who arent supposed to exist. the malevolence/ the deceit/ & manipulation exhibited by these five are simply reflections of the larger world they inhabit/ but do not participate in:

> sean
> contours of life unnoticed/

xv

michael
unrealized & suspect . . . our form is one of a bludgeoned thing/
wrapped in rhinestones & gauze/ blood almost sparklin/ a wildness
lurks always . . .

oppression/ makes us love one another badly/ makes our breathing
mangled/ while i am desperately trying to clear the air/
in the absence of extreme elegance/
madness can set right in like
a burnin gauloise on japanese silk.
though highly cultured/
even the silk must ask
how to burn up discreetly.

3/21/80 NYC

spell #7:

geechee jibara quik

magic trance manual for

technologically stressed

third world people

A THEATER PIECE

# CAST

*(in order of appearance)*

*lou*   a practicing magician

*alec*   a frustrated, angry actor's actor

*dahlia*   young gypsy (singer/dancer)

*eli*   a bartender who is also a poet

*bettina*   *dahlia*'s co-worker in a chorus

*lily*   an unemployed actress working as a barmaid

*natalie*   a not too successful performer

*ross*   guitarist-singer with *natalie*

*maxine*   an experienced actress


*this show is dedicated to my great aunt marie,*

*aunt lizzie, aunt jane and my grandma, viola benzena,*

*and her buddy, aunt effie, and the lunar year.*

*spell #7* was originally produced by Joseph Papp's New York Shakespeare Festival in New York City, 1979, with the following personnel:

Oz Scott, Director. Dianne McIntyre, Choreographer. Original Music by David Murray and Butch Morris. Scenery by Robert Yodice. Costumes by Grace Williams. Lighting by Victor En Yu Tan. With: Mary Alice, Avery Brooks, Laurie Carlos, Dyane Harvey, Larry Marshall, Reyno, La Tanya Richardson, Beth Shorter, and Ellis Williams. Jay Fernandez, Samuel L. Jackson, and Jack Landrón also appeared during the run.
Many thanks to Production Stage Manager, Jacqueline Yancey.

rtha Swope

opposite/ from prologue of spell #7, presented by the N.Y.S.F., the cast satirically celebrate their right to work in American theater, under the shadow of the great minstrel mask

above/ l. to r.: Dyane Harvey, Laurie Carlos, Reyno, Larry Marshall, La Tanya Richardson, Ellis.Williams, Beth Shorter in spell #7 at the N.Y.S.F., finally unmasked, the actors reveal themselves in their bar

# A C T   I

*(there is a huge black-face mask hanging from the ceiling of the theater as the audience enters. in a way the show has already begun, for the members of the audience must integrate this grotesque, larger than life misrepresentation of life into their pre-show chatter. slowly the house lights fade, but the mask looms even larger in the darkness.*

*once the mask is all that can be seen, lou, the magician, enters. he is dressed in the traditional costume of Mr. Interlocutor: tuxedo, bow-tie, top hat festooned with all kinds of whatnots that are obviously meant for good luck, he does a few catchy "soft-shoe" steps & begins singing a traditional version of a black play song)*

   lou (singing)
10 lil picaninnies all in bed
one fell out and the other nine said:
i sees yr hiney
all black & shiny
i see yr hiney
all black & shiny/ shiny

   *(as a greeting)*

yes/ yes/ yes     isnt life wonderful

   *(confidentially)*

my father is a retired magician
which accounts for my irregular behavior
everything comes outta magic hats
or bottles wit no bottoms & parakeets
are as easy to get as a couple a rabbits
or 3 fifty-cent pieces/ 1958
my daddy retired from magic & took
up another trade cuz this friend a mine
from the 3rd grade/ asked to be made white
on the spot

what cd any self-respectin colored american magician
do wit such an outlandish request/ cept
put all them razzamatazz hocus pocus zippity-doo-dah
thingamajigs away    cuz
colored chirren believin in magic

waz becomin politically dangerous for the race
& waznt nobody gonna be made white
on the spot just
from a clap of my daddy's hands
& the reason i'm so peculiar's
cuz i been studyin up on my daddy's technique
& everything i do is magic these days
& it's very colored/ very now you see it/ now you
dont mess wit me

    *(boastfully)*

                            i come from a family of retired
sorcerers/ active houngans & pennyante fortune tellers
wit 41 million spirits/ critturs & celestial bodies
on our side

               i'll listen to yr problems
               help wit yr career/ yr lover/ yr wanderin spouse
               make yr grandma's stay in heaven more
               gratifyin
               ease yr mother thru menopause & show yr son
               how to clean his room

*(while lou has been easing the audience into acceptance of his appearance & the
mask (his father, the ancestors, our magic), the rest of the company enters in tattered
fieldhand garb, blackface, and the countenance of stepan fetchit when he waz
frightened. their presence belies the magician's promise that "you'll be colored n love
it," just as the minstrel shows were lies, but lou continues)*

YES YES YES 3 wishes is all you get
   scarlet ribbons for yr hair
   a farm in mississippi
   someone to love you madly
all things are possible
but aint no colored magician in his right mind
gonna make you        white
i mean
       this is blk magic
you lookin at
& i'm fixin you up good/ fixin you up good & colored
& you gonna be colored all yr life
& you gonna love it/ bein colored/ all yr life/ colored & love it
love it/ bein colored. SPELL #7!

*(lou claps his hands, & the company which had been absolutely still til this moment/ jumps up. with a rhythm set on a washboard carried by one of them/ they begin a series of steps that identify every period of afro-american entertainment: from acrobats, comedians, tap-dancers, calindy dancers, cotton club choruses, apollo theatre du-wop groups, til they reach a frenzy in the midst of "hambone, hambone where ya been"/ & then take a bow à la bert williams/ the lights bump up abruptly.*

*the magician, lou, walks thru the black-faced figures in their kneeling poses, arms outstretched as if they were going to sing "mammy." he speaks now [as a companion of the mask] to the same audience who fell so easily into his hands & who were so aroused by the way the black-faced figures "sang n danced")*

### lou
why dont you go on & integrate a german-american school in st. louis mo./ 1955/ better yet why dont ya go on & be a red niggah in a blk school in 1954/ i got it/ try & make one friend at camp in the ozarks in 1957/ crawl thru one a jesse james' caves wit a class of white kids waitin outside to see the whites of yr eyes/ why dontcha invade a clique of working class italians trying to be protestant in a jewish community/ & come up a spade/ be a lil too dark/ lips a lil too full/ hair entirely too nappy/ to be beautiful/ be a smart child trying to be dumb/ you go meet somebody who wants/ always/ a lil less/ be cool when yr body says hot/ & more/ be a mistake in racial integrity/ an error in white folks' most absurd fantasies/ be a blk kid in 1954/ who's not blk enuf to lovingly ignore/ not beautiful enuf to leave alone/ not smart enuf to move outta the way/ not bitter enuf to die at an early age/ why dontchu c'mon & live my life for me/ since the dreams aint enuf/ go on & live my life for me/ i didnt want certain moments at all/ i'd give em to anybody . . . awright. alec.

*(the black-faced alec gives his minstrel mask to lou when he hears his name/ alec rises. the rest of the company is intimidated by this figure daring to talk without the protection of black-face. they move away from him/ or move in place as if in mourning)*

### alec
st. louis/ such a colored town/ a whiskey black space of history & neighborhood/ forever ours to lawrenceville/ where the only road open to me waz cleared by colonial slaves/ whose children never moved/ never seems like mended the torments of the Depression or the stains of demented spittle/ dropped from the lips of crystal women/ still makin independence flags/
st. louis/ on a halloween's eve to the veiled prophet/ usurpin the mystery of mardi gras/ i made it mine tho the queen waz always fair/ that

parade of pagan floats & tambourines/ commemorates me/ unlike the
lonely walks wit liberal trick or treaters/ back to my front door/ bag half
empty/

my face enuf to scare anyone i passed/ gee/ a colored kid/ whatta gas.
here/ a tree/ wanderin the horizon/ dipped in blues/ untended bones/
usedta hugs drawls rhythm & decency here a tree/ waitin to be hanged

sumner high school/ squat & pale on the corner/ like our vision waz to
be vague/ our memory of the war/ that made us free/ to be forgotten/
becomin paler/ linear movement from sous' carolina to missouri/
freedmen/ landin in jackie wilson's yelp/ daughters of the manumitted
swimmin in tina turner's grinds/ this is chuck berry's town disavowin
miscega-nation/ in any situation/ & they let us be/ electric blues & bo
didley/ the rockin pneumonia & boogie-woogie flu/ the slop & short fried
heads/ runnin always to the river chambersburg/ lil italy/ i passed
everyday at the sweet shoppe/ & waz afraid/ the cops raided truants/
regularly/ & after dark i wd not be seen wit any other colored/ sane &
lovin my life

(shouts n cries that are those of a white mob are heard, very loud . . . the still black-
faced figures try to move away from the menacing voices & memories)

voices
hey niggah/ over here

alec
behind the truck lay five hands claspin chains

voices
hey niggah/ over here

alec
round the trees/ 4 more sucklin steel

voices
hey niggah/ over here

alec
this is the borderline

voices
hey niggah/ over here

alec
a territorial dispute

10/

*voices*
hey niggah/ over here

    *alec (crouched on floor)*
cars loaded with families/ fellas from the factory/
one or two practical nurses/ become our trenches/
some dig into cement wit elbows/ under engines/
do not be seen in yr hometown
after sunset/ we suck up our shadows

      *(finally moved to tear off their "shadows," all but two of the company leave with*
      *their true faces bared to the audience. dahlia has, as if by some magical cause, shed*
      *not only her mask, but also her hideous overalls & picaninny-buckwheat wig, to*
      *reveal a finely laced unitard/ the body of a modern dancer. she throws her mask to*
      *alec, who tosses it away. dahlia begins a lyrical but pained solo as alec speaks for*
      *them)*

    *alec*
we will stand here
our shoulders embrace an enormous spirit
my dreams waddle in my lap
run round to miz bertha's
where lil richard gets his process
run backward to the rosebushes
& a drunk man lyin
down the block to the nuns
in pink habits/ prayin in a pink chapel
my dreams run to meet aunt marie
my dreams haunt me like the little geechee river
our dreams draw blood from old sores
this is our space
we are not movin

      *(dahlia finishes her movement/ alec is seen reaching for her/ lights out. in the*
      *blackout they exit as lou enters. lights come up on lou who repeats bitterly his*
      *challenge to the audience)*

    *lou*
why dontchu go on & live my life for me
i didnt want certain moments at all
i'd give them to anybody

      *(lou waves his hand commanding the minstrel mask to disappear, which it does. he*
      *signals to his left & again by magic, the lights come up higher revealing the interior of*

this is . . .

    *eli*
MY kingdom.
there shall be no trespassers/ no marauders
no tourists in my land
you nurture these gardens      or      be shot on sight
carelessness & other priorities
are not permitted within these walls
i am mantling an array of strength & beauty
no one shall interfere with this
the construction of myself
my city      my theater
my bar      come to my poems
but understand we speak english carefully
& perfect antillean french
our toilets are disinfected
the plants here sing to me each morning
come to my kitchen my parlor even my bed
i sleep on satin      surrounded by hand made
infants who bring me good luck & warmth
come even to my door
the burglar alarm/ armed guards vault from the east side
if i am in danger      a siren shouts
you are welcome
to my kingdom      my city    my self
but yr presence must not disturb these inhabitants
leave nothing out of place/ push no dust under my rugs
leave not a crack in my wine glasses
no finger prints
clean up after yrself in the bathroom
there are no maids here      no days off
for healing      no insurance policies
for dislocation of the psyche

aliens/ foreigners/ are granted resident status
we give them a little green card
as they prove themselves non-injurious
to the joy of my nation
i sustain no intrusions/ no double-entendre romance
no soliciting of sadness       in my life
are those who love me well
the rest are denied their visas . . .
is everyone ready to boogie

> *(finally, when eli calls for a boogie, the company does a dance that indicates these*
> *people have worked & played together a long time. as dance ends, the company sits &*
> *chats at the tables & at the bar. this is now a safe haven for these "minstrels" off from*
> *work. here they are free to be themselves, to reveal secrets, fantasies, nightmares, or*
> *hope. it is safe because it is segregated & magic reigns.*
>
> *lili, the waitress, is continually moving abt the bar, taking orders for drinks &*
> *generally staying on top of things)*

*alec*
gimme a triple bourbon/ & a glass of angel dust
these thursday nite audiences are abt to kill me

> *(eli goes behind bar to get drinks)*

*dahlia*
why do i drink so much?

*bettina, lily, natalie (in unison)*
who cares?

*dahlia*
but i'm an actress. i have to ask myself these questions

*lily*
that's a good reason to drink

*dahlia*
no/ i mean the character/ alec, you're a director/ give me some motivation

*alec*
motivation/ if you didn't drink you wd remember that you're not workin

*lily*
i wish i cd get just one decent part

lou
say as lady macbeth or mother courage

eli
how the hell is she gonna play lady macbeth and macbeth's a white dude?

lily
ross & natalie/ why are you countin pennies like that?

natalie
we had to wait on our money again

ross
and then we didnt get it

bettina
maybe they think we still accept beads & ribbons

natalie
i had to go around wit my tambourine just to get subway fare

eli
dont worry abt it/ have one on me

natalie
thank you eli

bettina (falling out of her chair)
oh . . .

alec
cut her off eli/ dont give her no more

lily
what's the matter bettina/ is yr show closin?

bettina (gets up, resets chair)
no/ my show is not closin/ but if that director asks me to play it any
blacker/ i'm gonna have to do it in a mammy dress

lou
you know/ countin pennies/ lookin for parts/ breakin tambourines/ we
must be outta our minds for doin this

*bettina*
no we're not outta our minds/ we're just sorta outta our minds

*lily*
no/ we're not outta our minds/ we've been doing this shit a long time . . .
ross/ captain theophilis conneau/ in *a slaver's logbook*/ says that "youths
of both sexes wear rings in the nose and lower lip and stick porcupine
quills thru the cartilage of the ear." ross/ when ringlin' bros. comes to
madison square garden/ dontcha know the white people just go

*ross*
in their cb radios

*dahlia*
in their mcdonald's hats

*eli*
with their save america t-shirts & those chirren who score higher on IQ
tests for the white chirren who speak english

*alec*
when the hockey games absorb all america's attention in winter/ they go
with their fists clenched & their tongues battering their women who dont
know a puck from a 3-yr-old harness racer

*bettina*
they go & sweat in fierce anger

*ross*
these factories

*natalie*
these middle management positions

*ross*
make madison square garden

*bettina*
the temple of the primal scream

(lily gets money from cash register & heads toward jukebox)

*lily*
oh how they love blood

15/

natalie
& how they dont even dress for the occasion/ all inconspicuous & pink

eli
now if willie colon come there

bettina
if/ we say/ the fania all stars gonna be there
in that nasty fantasy of the city council

ross
where the hot dogs are not even hebrew national

lily
and the bread is stale

ross
even in such a place where dance is an obscure notion

bettina
where one's joy is good cause for a boring chat with the pinkerton guard

dahlia
where the halls lead nowhere

eli
& "back to yr seat/ folks"

lily
when all one's budget for cruisin

lou
one's budget for that special dinner with you know who

lily
the one you wd like to love you

bettina
when yr whole reasonable allowance for leisure activity/
buys you a seat where what's goin on dont matter

dahlia
cuz you so high up/ you might be in seattle

16/

*lily*
even in such a tawdry space

*eli*
where vorster & his pals wd spit & expect black folks to lick it up

*ross (stands on chair)*
in such a place i've seen miracles

*all*
oh yeah/ aw/ ross

*ross*
the miracles

("music for the love of it," by butch morris, comes up on the jukebox/ this is a catchy
uptempo rhythm & blues post WW II. as they speak the company does a dance that
highlights their ease with one another & their familiarity with "all the new dance
steps")

*lily*
the commodores

*dahlia*
muhammad ali

*natalie*
bob marley

*alec*
& these folks who upset alla 7th avenue with their glow/
how the gold in their braids is new in this world of hard hats & men with
the grace of wounded buffalo/ how these folks in silk & satin/ in bodies
reekin of good love comin/ these pretty muthafuckahs

*dahlia*
make this barn

*lily*
this insult to good taste

*bettina*
a foray into paradise

*dahlia, lily, alec, natalie, & ross (in unison)*
we dress up

*bettina, eli, & lou (in unison)*
we dress up

*dahlia*
cuz we got good manners

*ross*
cd you really ask dr. funkenstein to come all that way & greet him in the
clothes you sweep yr kitchen in?

*all*
NO!

*bettina*
cd you say to muhammad ali/ well/ i just didnt have a chance to change/
you see i have a job/ & then i went jogging & well, you know its just
madison square garden

*lou*
my dear/ you know that wont do

*natalie*
we honor our guests/ if it costs us all we got

*dahlia*
when stevie wonder sings/ he don't want us lookin like we ain't got no
common sense/ he wants us to be as lovely as we really are/ so we strut &
reggae

*eli*
i seen some doing the jump up/ i myself just got happy/ but i'm tellin you
one thing for sure

*lily*
we fill up where we at

*bettina*
no police

*natalie*
no cheap beer

*dahlia*
no nasty smellin bano

*ross*
no hallways fulla derelicts & hustlers

*natalie*
gonna interfere wit alla this beauty

*alec*
if it wasnt for us/ in our latino chic/ our rasta-fare our outer space funk
suits & all the rest i have never seen

*bettina*
tho my daddy cd tell you bout them fox furs & stacked heels/ the
diamonds & marie antoinette wigs

*eli*
it's not cuz we got money

*natalie*
it's not cuz if we had money we wd spend it on luxury

*lily*
it's just when you gotta audience with the pope/ you look yr best

*bettina*
when you gonna see the queen of england/ you polish yr nails

*natalie*
when you gonna see one of them/ & you know who i mean

*alec*
they gotta really know

*bettina*
we gotta make em feel

*eli*
we dont do this for any old body

*lou*
we're doin this for you

19/

*natalie*
we dress up

*alec*
is our way of sayin/ you gettin the very best

*dahlia*
we cant do less/ we love too much to be stingy

*ross*
they give us too much to be loved ordinary

*lily*
we simply have good manners

*ross*
& an addiction to joy

*female cast members (in unison)*
WHEE . . .

*dahlia*
we dress up

*male cast members (in unison)*
HEY . . .

*bettina*
we gotta show the world/ we gotta corner on the color

*ross*
happiness just jumped right outta us/ & we are lookin good

(everyone in the bar is having so much fun/ that maxine takes on an exaggerated character as she enters/ in order to bring them to attention. the company freezes, half in respect/ half in parody)

*maxine*
cognac!

(the company relaxes, goes to tables or the bar. in the meantime, ross has remained in the spell of the character that maxine had introduced when she came in. he goes over to maxine who is having a drink/ & begins an improvisation)

*20/*

ross

she left the front gate open/ not quite knowing she wanted someone to
walk on thru the wrought iron fence/ scrambled in whiskey bottles broken
round old bike spokes/ some nice brown man to wind up in her bed/ she
really didnt know/ the sombrero that enveloped her face was a lil too
much for an april nite on the bowery/ & the silver halter dug out from
summer cookouts near riis beach/ didnt sparkle with the intensity of her
promise to have one good time/ before the children came back from
carolina. brooklyn cd be such a drag. every street cept flatbush & nostrand/
reminiscent of europe during the plague/ seems like nobody but sickness
waz out walkin/ drivels & hypes/ a few youngsters lookin for more than
they cd handle/ & then there waz fay/

(maxine rises, begins acting the story out)

waitin for a cab. anyone of the cars inchin along the boulevard cd see fay
waznt no whore/ just a good clean woman out for the nite/ & tho her left
titty jumped out from under her silver halter/ she didnt notice cuz she
waz lookin for a cab. the dank air fondled her long saggin bosom like a
possible companion/ she felt good. she stuck her tin-ringed hand on her
waist & watched her own ankles dance in the nite. she waz gonna have a
good time tonight/ she waz awright/ a whole lotta woman/ wit that special
brooklyn bottom strut. knowin she waznt comin in til dawn/ fay covered
herself/ sorta/ wit a light kacky jacket that just kept her titties from rompin
in the wind/ & she pulled it closer to her/ the winds waz comin/ from
nowhere jabbin/ & there waznt no cabs/ the winds waz beatin her behind/
whisperin/ gigglin/ you aint goin noplace/ you an ol bitch/ shd be at home
wit ur kids. fay beat off the voices/ & an EBONY-TRUE-TO-YOU cab
climbed the curb to get her. (as cabdriver)
     hope you aint plannin on stayin in brooklyn/ after 8:00 you dead in
brooklyn. (as narrator)
     she let her titty shake like she thot her mouth oughtta bubble like/ wd
she take off her panties/ i'd take her anywhere.

maxine (as if in cab)
i'm into havin a good time/ yr arms/ veins burstin/ like you usedta lift
tobacco onto trucks or cut cane/ i want you to be happy/ long as we dont
haveta stay in brooklyn

ross
& she made like she waz gypsy rose lee/ or the hotsy totsy girls in the
carnival round from waycross/ when it waz segregated

21/

        maxine
what's yr name?

        ross
my name is raphael

        maxine
oh that's nice

        ross
& fay moved where i cd see her out the rear view mirror/ waz tellin me all
bout her children & big eddie who waz away/ while we crossed the
manhattan bridge/ i kept smilin. (as cabdriver) where exactly you goin?

        maxine
i dont really know. i just want to have a good time. take me where i can
see famous people/ & act bizarre like sinatra at the kennedys/ maybe even
go round & beat up folks like jim brown/ throw somebody offa balcony/
you know/ for a good time

        ross
the only place i knew/ i took her/ after i kisst the spaces she'd been layin
open to me. fay had alla her $17 cuz i hadnt charged her nothin/ turned
the meter off/ said it waz wonderful to pick up a lady like her on atlantic
avenue/ i saw nobody but those goddamn whores/ & fay

        (maxine moves in to ross & gives him a very long kiss)

now fay waz a gd clean woman/ & she waz burstin with pride &
enthusiasm when she walked into the place where I swore/ all the
actresses & actors hung out

        (the company joins in ross' story; responding to maxine as tho she waz entering their
        bar)

oh yes/ there were actresses in braids & lipstick/ wigs & winged tip
pumps/ fay assumed the posture of someone she'd always admired/ etta
james/ the waitress asked her to leave cuz she waz high/ & fay knew better
than that

        maxine (responding to lily's indication of throwing her out)
i aint high/ i'm enthusiastic/ and i'm gonna have me a goooooooood/ ol
time

*ross*

she waz all dressed up/ she came all the way from brooklyn/ she must
look high cuz i/ the taxi-man/ well i got her a lil excited/ that waz all/ but
she waz gonna cool out/ cuz she waz gonna meet her friends/ at this place/
yes. she knew that/ & she pushed a bunch of rhododendrum/ outta her
way so she cd get over to that table/ & stood over the man with the biggest
niggah eyes & warmest smellin mouth

*maxine*

please/ let me join you/ i come all the way from brooklyn/ to have a good
time/ you dont think i'm high do ya/ cd i please join ya/ i just wanna have
a good ol time

*ross (as bettina turns away)*

the woman sipped chablis & looked out the window hopin to see one of
the bowery drunks fall down somewhere/ fay's voice hoverin/ flirtin wit
hope

*lou (turning to face maxine)*

why dont you go downstairs & put yr titty in yr shirt/ you cant have no
good time lookin like that/ now go on down & then come up & join us

*(bettina & lou rise & move to another table)*

*ross*

fay tried to shove her flesh anywhere/ she took off her hat/ bummed a
kool/ swallowed somebody's cognac/ & sat down/ waitin/ for a gd time

*maxine (rises & hugs ross)*

aw ross/ when am i gonna get a chance to feel somethin like that/ i got
into this business cuz i wanted to feel things all the time/ & all they want
me to do is put my leg in my face/ smile/ &

*lily*

you better knock on some wood/ maxine/ at least yr workin

*bettina*

& at least yr not playin a whore/ if some other woman comes in here &
tells me she's playin a whore/ i think i might kill her

*eli*

you'd kill her so you cd say/ oh dahlia died & i know all her lines

*bettina*
aw hush up eli/ dnt you know what i mean?

*eli*
no miss/ i dont/ are you in the theater?

*bettina*
mr. bartender/ poet sir/ i am theater

*dahlia*
well miss theater/ that's a surprise/ especially since you fell all over the
damn stage in the middle of my solo

*lily*
she did

*eli*
miss theater herself fell down?

*dahlia*
yeah/ she cant figure out how to get attention without makin somebody
else look bad

*maxine*
now dahlia/ it waznt that bad/ i hardly noticed her

*dahlia*
it waz my solo/ you werent sposed to notice her at all!

*bettina*
you know dahlia/ i didnt do it on purpose/ i cda hurt myself

*dahlia*
that wd be unfortunate

*bettina*
well miss thing with those big ass hips you got/ i dont know why you
think you can do the ballet anyway

(the company breaks; they're expecting a fight)

*dahlia* (crossing to bettina)
i got this

*(demonstrates her leg extension)*

## & alla this

*(dahlia turns her back to bettina/ & slaps her own backside. bettina grabs dahlia, turns her around & they begin a series of finger snaps that are a paraphrase of ailey choreography for very dangerous fights. eli comes to break up the impending altercation)*

*eli*
## ladies ladies ladies

*(eli separates the two)*

*eli*
people keep tellin me to put my feet on the ground
i get mad & scream/ there is no ground
only shit pieces from dogs horses & men who dont live
anywhere/ they tell me think straight & make myself
somethin/ i shout & sigh/ i am a poet/ i write poems
i make words cartwheel & somersault down pages
outta my mouth come visions distilled like bootleg
whiskey/ i am like a radio but i am a channel of my own
i keep sayin i write poems/ & people keep askin me
what do i do/ what in the hell is going on?
people keep tellin me these are hard times/ what are
you gonna be doin ten years from now/
what in the hell do you think/ i am gonna be writin poems
i will have poems inchin up the walls of the lincoln tunnel/
i am gonna feed my children poems on rye bread with horseradish/
i am gonna send my mailman off with a poem for his wagon/
give my doctor a poem for his heart/ i am a poet/
i am not a part-time poet/ i am not a amateur poet/
i dont even know what that person cd be/ whoever that is
authorizing poetry as an avocation/ is a fraud/
put yr own feet on the ground

*bettina*
i'm sorry eli/ i just dont want to be a gypsy all my life

*(the bar returns to normal humming & sipping. the lights change to focus on lily/ who begins to say what's really been on her mind. the rest of the company is not aware of lily's private thoughts. only bettina responds to lily, but as a partner in fantasy, not as a voyeur)*

*lily (illustrating her words with movement)*
i'm gonna simply brush my hair. rapunzel pull yr tresses back into the
tower. & lady godiva give up horseback riding. i'm gonna alter my social &
professional life dramatically. i will brush 100 strokes in the morning/ 100
strokes midday & 100 strokes before retiring. i will have a very busy
schedule. between the local trains & the express/ i'm gonna brush. i brush
between telephone calls. at the disco i'm gonna brush on the slow songs/ i
dont slow dance with strangers. i'ma brush my hair before making love &
after. i'll brush my hair in taxis. while windowshopping. when i have
visitors over the kitchen table/ i'ma brush. i brush my hair while thinking
abt anything. mostly i think abt how it will be when i get my full heada
hair. like lifting my head in the morning will become a chore. i'll try to
turn my cheek & my hair will weigh me down

*(lily falls to the floor. bettina helps lift her to her knees, then begins to dance & mime
as lily speaks)*

i dream of chaka khan/ chocolate from graham central station with all
seven wigs/ & medusa. i brush & brush. i use olive oil hair food/ &
posner's vitamin E. but mostly i brush & brush. i may lose contact with
most of my friends. i cd lose my job/ but i'm on unemployment & brush
while waiting on line for my check. i'm sure i get good recommendations
from my social worker: such a fastidious woman/ that lily/ always
brushing her hair. nothing in my dreams suggests that hair brushing/ per
se/ has anything to do with my particular heada hair. a therapist might say
that the head fulla hair has to do with something else/ like: a symbol of
lily's unconscious desires. but i have no therapist

*(she takes imaginary pen from bettina, who was pretending to be a therapist/ & sits
down at table across from her)*

& my dreams mean things to me/ like if you dreamed abt tobias/ then
something has happened to tobias/ or he is gonna show up. if you dream
abt yr grandma who's dead/ then you must be doing something she doesnt
like/ or she wdnta gone to all the trouble to leave heaven like that. if you
dream something red/ you shd stop. if you dream something green/ you
shd keep doing it. if a blue person appears in yr dreams/ then that person
is yr true friend
   & that's how i see my dreams. & this head fulla hair i have in my
dreams is lavender & nappy as a 3-yr-old's in a apple tree. i can fry an egg
& see the white of the egg spreadin in the grease like my hair is gonna
spread in the air/ but i'm not egg-yolk yellow/ i am brown & the egg white

isnt white at all/ it is my actual hair/ & it wd go on & on forever/ irregular
like a rasta-man's hair. irregular/ gargantuan & lavender. nestled on blue
satin pillows/ pillows like the sky. & so i fry my eggs. i buy daisies dyed
lavender & laced lavender tablemats & lavender nail polish. though i
never admit it/ i really do believe in magic/ & can do strange things when
something comes over me. soon everything around me will be lavender/
fluffy & consuming. i will know not a moment of bitterness/ through all
the wrist aching & tennis elbow from brushing/ i'll smile. no regrets/ "je
ne regrette rien" i'll sing like edith piaf. when my friends want me to go
see tina turner or pacheco/ i'll croon "sorry/ i have to brush my hair."

i'll find ambrosia. my hair'll grow pomegranates & soil/ rich as round
the aswan/ i wake in my bed to bananas/ avocados/ collard greens/ the
tramps' latest disco hit/ fresh croissant/ pouilly fuissé/ ishmael reed's
essays/ charlotte carter's stories/ all stream from my hair.

& with the bricks that plop from where a 9-year-old's top braid wd be/
i will brush myself a house with running water & a bidet. i'll have a closet
full of clean bed linen & the lil girl from the castro convertible
commercial will come & open the bed repeatedly & stay on as a helper to
brush my hair. lily is the only person i know whose every word leaves a
purple haze on the tip of yr tongue. when this happens i says clouds are
forming/ & i has to close the windows. violet rain is hard to remove from
blue satin pillows

(lou, the magician, gets up. he points to lily sitting very still. he reminds us that it is
only thru him that we are able to know these people without the "masks"/ the lies/ &
he cautions that all their thoughts are not benign. they are not safe from what they
remember or imagine)


lou
you have t come with me/ to this place where magic is/
to hear my song/ some times i forget & leave my tune
in the corner of the closet under all the dirty clothes/
in this place/ magic asks me where i've been/ how i've
been singin/ lately i leave my self in all the wrong hands/
in this place where magic is involved in
undoin our masks/ i am able to smile & answer that.
in this place where magic always asks for me
i discovered a lot of other people who talk without mouths
who listen to what you say/ by watchin yr jewelry dance
& in this place where magic stays
you can let yrself in or out
but when you leave yrself at home/ burglars & daylight thieves
pounce on you & sell yr skin/ at cut-rates on tenth avenue

(ross has been playing the acoustic guitar softly as lou spoke. alec picks up on the
train of lou's thoughts & tells a story that in turn captures natalie's attention. slowly,
natalie becomes the woman alec describes)

alec

she had always wanted a baby/ never a family/ never a man/
she had always wanted a baby/ who wd suckle & sleep
a baby boy who wd wet/ & cry/ & smile
suckle & sleep
when she sat in bars/ on the stool/ near the door/ & cross from the juke
box/ with her legs straddled & revealin red lace pants/ & lil hair smashed
under the stockings/ she wd think how she wanted this baby & how she
wd call the baby/ "myself" & as she thot/ bout this brown lil thing/ she
ordered another bourbon/ double & tilted her head as if to cuddle some
infant/ not present/ the men in the bar never imagined her as someone's
mother/ she rarely tended her own self carefully/

(natalie rises slowly, sits astride on the floor)

just enough to exude a languid sexuality that teased the men off work/ &
the bartender/ ray who waz her only friend/ women didnt take to her/ so
she spent her afternoons with ray/ in the bar round the corner from her lil
house/ that shook winsomely in a hard wind/ surrounded by three weepin
willows

natalie

my name is sue-jean & i grew here/ a ordinary colored girl with no claims
to any thing/ or anyone/ i drink now/ bourbon/ in harder times/ beer/ but i
always wanted to have a baby/ a lil boy/ named myself

alec

one time/ she made it with ray

natalie

& there waz nothin special there/ only a hot rough bangin/ a brusque
barrelin throwin of torso/ legs & sweat/ ray wanted to kiss me/ but i
screamed/ cuz i didnt like kissin/ only fuckin/ & we rolled round/ i waz a
peculiar sorta woman/ wantin no kisses/ no caresses/ just power/ heat & no
eaziness of thrust/ ray pulled himself outa me/ with no particular
exclamation/ he smacked me on my behind/ i waz grinnin/ & he took that
as a indication of his skill/ he believed he waz a good lover/ & a woman
like me/ didnt never want nothin but a hard dick/ & everyone believed
that/ tho no one in town really knew

*alec*
so ray/ went on behind the bar cuz he had got his

*natalie*
& i lay in the corner laughin/ with my drawers/ twisted round my ankles &
my hair standin every which way/ i waz laughin/ knowin i wd have this
child/ myself/ & no one wd ever claim him/ cept me cuz i waz a low-down
thing/ layin in sawdust & whiskey stains/ i laughed & had a good time
masturbatin in the shadows.

*alec*
sue-jean ate starch for good luck

*natalie*
like mama kareena/ tol me

*alec*
& she planted five okras/ five collards/ & five tomatoes

*natalie*
for good luck too/ i waz gonna have this baby/ i even went over to the
hospital to learn prenatal care/ & i kept myself clean

*alec*
sue-jean's lanky body got ta spreadin & her stomach waz taut & round
high in her chest/ a high pregnancy is sure to be a boy/ & she smiled

*natalie*
i stopped goin to the bar

*alec*
started cannin food

*natalie*
knittin lil booties

*alec*
even goin to church wit the late nite radio evangelist

*natalie*
i gotta prayer cloth for the boy/ myself waz gonna be safe from all that his
mama/ waz prey to

*alec*

sure/ sue-jean waz a scandal/ but that waz to be expected/ cuz she waz
always a po criterish chile

*natalie*

& wont no man bout step my way/ ever/ just cuz i hadda bad omen on me/
from the very womb/ i waz bewitched is what the ol women usedta say

*alec*

sue-jean waz born on a full moon/ the year of the flood/ the night the river
raised her skirts & sat over alla the towns & settlements for 30 miles in
each direction/ the nite the river waz in labor/ gruntin & groanin/ splittin
trees & families/ spillin cupboards over the ground/ waz the nite sue-jean
waz born

*natalie*

& my mother died/ drownin/ holdin me up over the mud crawlin in her
mouth

*alec*

somebody took her & she lived to be the town's no one/ now with the boy
achin & dancin in her belly/ sue-jean waz a gay & gracious woman/ she
made pies/ she baked cakes & left them on the stoop of the church she had
never entered just cuz she wanted/ & she grew plants & swept her floors/
she waz someone she had never known/ she waz herself with child/ & she
waz a wonderful bulbous thing

*natalie*

the nite/ myself waz born/ ol mama kareena from the hills came down to
see bout me/ i hollered & breathed/ i did exactly like mama kareena said/
& i pushed & pushed & there waz a earthquake up in my womb/ i wanted
to sit up & pull the tons of logs trapped in my crotch out/ so i cd sleep/
but it wdnt go way/ i pushed & thot i saw 19 horses runnin in my pussy/ i
waz sure there waz a locomotive stalled up in there burnin coal & steamin
& pushin gainst a mountain

*alec*

finally the child's head waz within reach & mama kareena/ brought the
boy into this world

*natalie*

& he waz awright/ with alla his toes & his fingers/ his lil dick & eyes/
elbows that bent/ & legs/ straight/ i wanted a big glassa bourbon/ & mama

30/

kareena brought it/ right away/ we sat drinkin the bourbon/ & lookin at the child whose name waz myself/ like i had wanted/ & the two of us ate placenta stew . . . i waznt really sure . . .

*alec*
sue-jean you werent really sure you wanted myself to wake up/ you always wanted him to sleep/ or at most to nurse/ the nites yr dreams were disturbed by his cryin

*natalie*
i had no one to help me

*alec*
so you were always with him/ & you didnt mind/ you knew this waz yr baby/ myself/ & you cuddled him/ carried him all over the house with you all day/ no matter/ what

*natalie*
everythin waz going awright til/ myself wanted to crawl

*alec (moving closer to natalie)*
& discover a world of his own/ then you became despondent/ & yr tits began to dry & you lost the fullness of yr womb/ where myself/ had lived

*natalie*
i wanted that back

*alec*
you wanted back the milk

*natalie*
& the tight gourd of a stomach i had when myself waz bein in me

*alec*
so you slit his wrists

*natalie*
he waz sleepin

*alec*
sucked the blood back into yrself/ & waited/ myself shriveled up in his crib

31/

*natalie*
a dank lil blk thing/ i never touched him again

*alec*
you were always holdin yr womb/ feelin him kick & sing to you bout love/
& you wd hold yr tit in yr hand

*natalie*
like i always did when i fed him

*alec*
& you waited & waited/ for a new myself. tho there were labor pains

*natalie*
& i screamed in my bed

*alec*
yr legs pinnin to the air

*natalie*
spinnin sometimes like a ferris wheel/ i cd get no child to fall from me

*alec*
& she forgot abt the child bein born/ & waz heavy & full all her life/ with
"myself"

*natalie*
who'll be out/ any day now

(eli moves from behind the bar to help natalie/ or to clean tables. he doesnt really
know. he stops suddenly)

*eli*
aint that a goddamn shame/ aint that a way
to come into the world
sometimes i really cant write
sometimes i cant even talk

(the minstrel mask comes down very slowly. blackout, except for lights on the big
minstrel mask which remains visible throughout intermission)

# ACT II

*(all players onstage are frozen, except lou, who makes a motion for the big minstrel mask to disappear again. as the mask flies up, lou begins)*

### lou

in this place where magic stays
you can let yrself in or out

*(he makes a magic motion. a samba is heard from the jukebox & activity is begun in the bar again. dahlia, natalie & lily enter, apparently from the ladies room)*

### natalie

i swear we went to that audition in good faith/ & that man asked us where we learned to speak english so well/ i swear this foreigner/ asked us/ from the city of new york/ where we learned to speak english.

### lily

all i did was say "bom dia/ como vai"/ and the englishman got red in the face

### lou *(as the englishman)*

yr from the states/ aren't you?

### lily

"sim"/ i said/ in good portuguese

### lou

but you speak portuguese

### lily

"sim" i said/ in good portuguese

### lou

how did you pick that up?

### lily

i hadda answer so simple/ i cdnt say i learned it/ cuz niggahs cant learn & that wda been too hard on the man/ so i said/ in good english: i held my ear to the ground & listened to the samba from bêlim

### dahlia

you should have said: i make a lotta phone calls to casçais, portugao

*bettina*
i gotta bahiano boyfriend

*natalie*
how abt: i waz an angolan freedom fighter

*maxine*
no/ lily/ tell him: i'm a great admirer of zeza motto & leci brandao

*lily*
when the japanese red army invaded san juan/ they poisoned the papaya
with portuguese. i eat a lotta papaya. last week/ i developed a strange
schizophrenic condition/ with 4 manifest personalities: one spoke english
& understood nothing/ one spoke french & had access to the world/ one
spoke spanish & voted against statehood for puerto rico/ one spoke
portuguese. "eu naõ falo ingles entaõ y voce"/ i dont speak english
anymore/ & you?

*(all the women in the company have been doing samba steps as the others spoke/ now
they all dance around a table in their own ritual/ which stirs alec & lou to interrupt
this female segregation. the women scatter to different tables, leaving the two
interlopers alone. so, alec & lou begin their conversation)*

*alec*
not only waz she without a tan, but she held her purse close to her hip
like a new yorker. someone who rode the paris métro or listened to
mariachis in plaza santa cecilia. she waz not from here

*(he sits at table)*

*lou (following suit)*
but from there

*alec*
some there where coloureds/ mulattoes/ negroes/ blacks cd make a living
big enough to leave there to come here/ where no one went there much
any more for all sorts of reasons

*lou*
the big reasons being immigration restrictions & unemployment.
nowadays, immigration restrictions of every kind apply to any non-
european persons who want to go there from here

*alec*
some who want to go there from here risk fetching trouble with the
customs authority there

*lou*
or later with the police, who can tell who's not from there cuz the shoes
are pointed & laced strange

*alec*
the pants be for august & yet it's january

*lou*
the accent is patterned for pétionville, but working in crown heights

*alec*
what makes a person comfortably ordinary here cd make him dangerously
conspicuous there.

*lou*
so some go to london or amsterdam or paris/ where they are so abounding
no one tries to tell who is from where

*alec*
still the far right wing of every there prints lil pamphlets that say
everyone from there shd leave & go back where they came from

*lou*
this is manifest legally thru immigration restrictions & personally thru
unemployment

*alec*
anyway the yng woman waz from there/ & she waz alone. that waz good.
cuz if a person had no big brother in gronigen/ no aunt in rouen

*lou*
no sponsor in chicago

*alec*
this brown woman from there might be a good idea. everybody in the
world/ european & non-european alike/ everybody knows that rich white
girls are hard to find. some of them joined the weather underground/ some
the baader-meinhof gang.

35/

*lou*
a whole bunch of them gave up men entirely


*alec*
so the exotic lover in the sun routine becomes more difficult to swing/ if
she wants to talk abt plastic explosives & the resistance of the black
masses to socialism/ instead of giving head as the tide slips in or lending
money


*lou*
just for the next few days


*alec*
is hard to find a rich white girl who is so dumb/ too


*lou*
anyway. the whole world knows/ european & non-european alike/ the
whole world knows that nobody loves the black woman like they love
farrah fawcett-majors. the whole world dont turn out for a dead black
woman like they did for marilyn monroe.


*alec*
actually/ the demise of josephine baker waz an international event


*lou*
but she waz a war hero
the worldwide un-beloved black woman is a good idea/ if she is from
there & one is a young man with gd looks/ piercing eyes/ & knowledge of
several romantic languages


   *(throughout this conversation, alec & lou will make attempts to seduce, cajole, & woo
   the women of the bar as their narrative indicates. the women play the roles as
   described, being so moved by romance)*


*alec*
the best dancing spots/ the hill where one can see the entire bay at
twilight


*lou*
the beach where the seals & pelicans run free/ the hidden "local"
restaurants

*alec*
"aw babee/ you so pretty" begins often in the lobby of hotels where the
bright handsome yng men wd be loiterers

*lou*
were they not needed to tend the needs of the black women from there

*alec*
tourists are usually white people or asians who didnt come all this way to
meet a black woman who isnt even foreign

*lou*
so hotel managers wink an eye at the yng men in the lobby or by the bar
who wd be loitering/ but are gonna help her have a gd time

*alec*
maybe help themselves too

*lou*
everybody in the world/ european & non-european alike/ everybody
knows the black woman from there is not treated as a princess/ as a jewel/
a cherished lover

*alec*
that's not how sapphire got her reputation/ nor how mrs. jefferson
perceives the world

*lou*
you know/ babee/ you dont act like them. aw babee/ you so pretty

*alec*
the yng man in the hotel watches the yng blk woman sit & sit & sit/ while
the european tourists dance with each other/ & the dapper local fellas
mambo frenetically with secretaries from arizona/ in search of the missing
rich white girl. our girl sits &

*female cast members (in unison)*
sits & sits & sits

*alec (to dahlia & natalie, who move to the music)*
maybe she is courageous & taps her foot. maybe she is bold & enjoys the
music/ smiling/ shaking shoulders. let her sit & let her know she is
unwanted

lou
she is not white & she is not from here

alec
let her know she is not pretty enuf to dance the next merengue. then
appear/ mysteriously/ in the corner of the bar. stare at her. just stare. when
stevie wonder's song/ "isnt she lovely"/ blares thru the red-tinted light/
ask her to dance & hold her as tyrone power wda. hold her & stare

(ross & eli sing the chorus to stevie wonder's "isn't she lovely")

lou
dance yr ass off. she has been discovered by the non-european fred astaire

alec
let her know she is a surprise/ an event. by the look on yr face you've
never seen anyone like this black woman from there. you say: "aw/ you
not from here?"/ totally astonished. she murmurs that she is from there. as
if to apologize for her unfortunate place of birth

lou
you say

alec
aw babee/ you so pretty. & it's all over

lou
a night in a pension near the sorbonne. pick her up from the mattress.
throw her gainst the wall in a show of exotic temper & passion:
"maintenant/ tu es ma femme. nous nous sommes mariés." unions of this
sort are common wherever the yng black women travel alone. a woman
traveling alone is an affront to the non-european man who is known the
world over/ to european & non-european alike/ for his way with women

alec
his sense of romance/ how he can say:

lou
aw babee/ you so pretty . . . and even a beautiful woman will believe no
one else ever recognized her loveliness

eli
or else/ he comes to a cafe in willemstad in the height of the sunset. an
able-bodied/ sinewy yng man who wants to buy one beer for the yng

woman. after the first round/ he discovers he has run out of money/ so she
must buy the next round/ when he discovers/ what beautiful legs you
have/ how yr mouth is like the breath of tiger lilies. we shall make love in
the/ how you call it/ yes in the earth/ in the dirt/ i will have you in my/
how you say/ where things grow/ aw/ yes/ i will have you in the soil.
probably under the stars & smelling of wine/ an unforgettable
international affair can be consummated

(the company sings "tara's theme" as eli ends his speech. eli & bettina take a tango
walk to the bar, while maxine mimics a 1930's photographer, shooting them as they
sail off into the sunset)

maxine
at 11:30 one evening i waz at the port authority/ new york/ united states/
myself. now i waz there & i spoke english & waz holding approximately
$7 american currency/ when a yng man from there came up to me from
the front of the line of people waiting for the princeton new jersey united
states local bus. i mean to say/ he gave up his chance for a good seat to
come say to me:

ross
i never saw a black woman reading nietzsche

maxine
i waz demure enough/ i said i have to for a philosophy class. but as the
night went on i noticed this yng man waz so much like the other yng men
from here/ who use their bodies as bait & their smiles as passport
alternatives. anyway the night did go on. we were snuggled together in the
rear of the bus going down the jersey turnpike. he told me in english/ that
he had spoken all his life in st. louis/ where he waz raised:

ross
i've wanted all my life to meet someone like you. i want you to meet my
family/ who haven't seen me in a long time/ since i left missouri looking
for opportunity . . .

(he is lost for words)

lou (stage whisper)
opportunity to sculpt

ross
thank you/ opportunity to sculpt

39 /

   *maxine*
he had been everyplace/ he said

   *ross*
you arent like any black woman i've ever met anywhere

   *maxine*
here or there

   *ross*
i had to come back to new york cuz of immigration restrictions & high
unemployment among black american sculptors abroad

   *maxine*
just as we got to princeton/ he picked my face up from his shoulder &
said:

   *ross*
aw babee/ you so pretty

   *maxine*
aw babee/ you so pretty. i believe that night i must have looked beautiful
for a black woman from there/ though i cd be asked at any moment to tour
the universe/ to climb a 6-story walkup with a brilliant & starving painter/
to share kadushi/ to meet mama/ to getta kiss each time the swing falls
toward the willow branch/ to imagine where he say he from/ & more. i cd/
i cd have all of it/ but i cd not be taken/ long as i don't let a stranger be
the first to say:

   *lou*
aw babee/ you so pretty

   *maxine*
after all/ immigration restrictions & unemployment cd drive a man to
drink or to lie

   *(she breaks away from ross)*

so if you know yr beautiful & bright & cherishable awready/ when he say/
in whatever language:

   *alec (to natalie)*
aw babee/ you so pretty

   **40/**

*maxine*
you cd say:

*natalie*
i know. thank you

*maxine*
then he'll smile/ & you'll smile. he'll say:

*eli (stroking bettina's thigh)*
what nice legs you have

*maxine*
you can say:

*bettina (removing his hand)*
yes. they run in the family

*maxine*
oh! whatta universe of beautiful & well traveled women!

*male cast members (in unison)*
aw babee/ i've never met anyone like you

*female cast members (in unison, pulling away from men to stage
edges)*
that's strange/ there are millions of us!

*(men all cluster after unsuccessful attempts to persuade their women to talk. alec gets
the idea to serenade the women; ross takes the first verse, with men singing back-up.
song is "ooh baby," by smokey robinson)*

*ross (singing)*
i did you wrong/ my heart went out to play/ but in the game
i lost you/ what a price to pay/ i'm cryin . . .

*male players (singing)*
oo oo oo/ baby baby. . . . oo oo oo/ baby baby

*(this brings no response from the women; the men elect eli to lead the second verse)*

*eli*
mistakes i know i've made a few/ but i'm only human

you've made mistakes too/ i'm cryin . . .
oo oo oo/ baby baby . . . oo oo oo/ baby baby

*(the women slowly forsake their staunch indignation/ returning to the arms of their*
*partners. all that is except lily, who walks abt the room of couples awkwardly)*

*male cast members & lily (singing)*
i'm just about at the end of my rope
but i can't stop trying/ i cant give up hope
cause i/ i believe one day/ i'll hold you near
whisper i love you/ until that day is here
i'm cryin . . . oo oo oo/ baby baby

*(lily begins as the company continues to sing)*

*lily*
unfortunately
the most beautiful man in the world
is unavailable
    that's what he told me
i saw him wandering abt/ said well this is one of a kind
& i might be able to help him out
so alone & pretty in all this ganja & bodies melting
he danced with me & i cd become that
a certain way to be held that's considered in advance
a way a thoughtful man wd kiss a woman who
cd be offended easily/ but waznt cuz
of course the most beautiful man in the world
knows exactly what to do
with someone who knows that's who he is/
these dreads fallin thru my dress
so my nipples just stood up
these hands playin the guitar on my back
the lips somewhere between my neck
& my forehead
talking bout ocho rios & how i really must go
marcus garvey cda come in the door & we/
we wd still be dancin that dance
the motion that has more to do with kinetic energy
than shootin stars/ more to do with the impossibility
of all this/ & how it waz awready bein too much
our reason failed
we tried to go away & be just together

aside from the silence that weeped
with greed/ we didnt need/ anything/ but one another
for tonite
but he is the most beautiful man in the world
    says he's unavailable/
& this man whose eyes made me
half-naked & still & brazen/ was singin with me
since we cd not talk/ we sang

(*male players end their chorus with a flourish*)

*lily*
we sang with bob marley
this man/ surely the most beautiful man in the world/ & i
sang/ "i wanna love you & treat you right/

(*the couples begin different kinds of reggae dances*)

i wanna love you every day & every nite"

*the company (dancing & singing)*
we'll be together with the roof right over our heads
we'll share the shelter of my single bed
we'll share the same room/ jah provide the bread

*dahlia (stops dancing during conversation)*
i tell you it's not just the part that makes me love you so much

*lou*
what is it/ wait/ i know/ you like my legs

*dahlia*
yes/ uh huh/ yr legs & yr arms/ & . . .

*lou*
but that's just my body/ you started off saying you loved me & now i see
it's just my body
                                            /

*dahlia*
oh/ i didnt mean that/ it's just i dont know you/ except as the character
i'm sposed to love/ & well i know rehearsal is over/ but i'm still in love
with you

(*they go to the bar to get drinks, then sit at a table*)

*ross*
but baby/ you have to go on the road. we need the money

*natalie*
i'm not going on the road so you can fuck all these aspiring actresses

*ross*
aw/ just some of them/ baby

*natalie*
that's why i'm not going

*ross*
if you dont go on the road i'll still be fuckin em/ but you & me/ we'll be in trouble/ you understand?

*natalie (stops dancing)*
no i dont understand

*ross*
well let me break it down to you

*natalie*
please/ break it down to me

*bettina (stops dancing)*
hey/ natalie/ why dont you make him go on the road/ they always want us to be so goddamned conscientious

*alec (stops dancing)*
dont you think you shd mind yr own bizness?

*natalie*
yeah bettina/ mind yr own bizness

(she pulls ross to a table with her)

*bettina (to alec)*
no/ i'm tired of having to take any & every old job to support us/ & you get to have artistic integrity & refuse parts that are beneath you

*alec*
thats right/ i'm not playing the fool or the black buck pimp circus/ i'm an

44/

actor not a stereotype/ i've been trained. you know i'm a classically
trained actor

    *bettina*
& just what do you think we are?

    *maxine*
well/ i got offered another whore part downtown

    *eli*
you gonna take it?

    *maxine*
yeah

    *lily*
if you dont/ i know someone who will

    *alec (to bettina)*
i told you/ we arent gonna get anyplace/ by doin every bit part for a
niggah that someone waves in fronta my face

    *bettina*
& we arent gonna live long on nothin/ either/ cuz i'm quittin my job

    *alec*
be in the real world for once & try to understand me

    *bettina*
you mean/ i shd understand that you are the great artist & i'm the trouper.

    *alec*
i'm not sayin that we cant be gigglin & laughin all the time dancin
around/ but i cant stay in these "hate whitey" shows/ cuz they arent true

    *bettina*
a failure of imagination on yr part/ i take it

    *alec*
no/ an insult to my person

    *bettina*
oh i see/ you wanna give the people some more make-believe

45/

*alec*

i cd always black up again & do minstrel work/ wd that make you happy?

*bettina*

there is nothin niggardly abt a decent job. work is honorable/ work!

*alec*

well/ i got a problem. i got lots of problems/ but i got one i want you to fix
& if you can fix it/ i'll do anything you say. last spring this niggah from
the midwest asked for president carter to say he waz sorry for that
forgettable phenomenon/ slavery/ which brought us all together. i never
did get it/ none of us ever got no apology from no white folks abt not bein
considered human beings/ that makes me mad & tired. someone told me
"roots" was the way white folks worked out their guilt/ the success of
"roots" is the way white folks assuaged their consciences/ i dont know
this/ this is what i waz told. i dont get any pleasure from nobody watchin
me trying to be a slave i once waz/ who got away/ when we all know they
had an emancipation proclamation/ that the civil war waz not fought over
us. we all know that we/ actually dont exist unless we play football or
basketball or baseball or soccer/ pélé/ see they still import a strong niggah
to earn money. art here/ isnt like in the old country/ where we had some
spare time & did what we liked to do/ i dont know this either/ this is also
something i've been told. i just want to find out why no one has even
been able to sound a gong & all the reporters recite that the gong is ringin/
while we watch all the white people/ immigrants & invaders/
conquistadors & relatives of london debtors from georgia/ kneel &
apologize to us/ just for three or four minutes. now/ this is not impossible/
& someone shd make a day where a few minutes of the pain of our lives is
acknowledged. i have never been very interested in what white people
did/ cuz i waz able/ like most of us/ to have very lil to do with them/ but
if i become a success that means i have to talk to white folks more than in
high school/ they are everywhere/ you know how they talk abt a
neighborhood changin/ we suddenly become all over the place/ they are
now all over my life/ & i dont like it. i am not talkin abt poets & painters/
not abt women & lovers of beauty/ i am talkin abt that proverbial white
person who is usually a man who just/ turns yr body around/ looks at yr
teeth & yr ass/ who feels yr calves & back/ & agrees on a price. we are/ you
see/ now able to sell ourselves/ & i am still a person who is tired/ a person
who is not into his demise/ just three minutes for our lives/ just three
minutes of silence & a gong in st. louis/ oakland/ in los angeles . . .

*(the entire company looks at him as if he's crazy/ he tries to leave the bar/ but bettina
stops him)*

46/

*bettina*

you're still outta yr mind. ain't no apologies keeping us alive.

*lou*

what are you gonna do with white folks kneeling all over the country
anyway/ man

*(lou signals everyone to kneel)*

*lily*

they say i'm too light to work/ but when i asked him what he meant/ he
said i didnt actually look black. but/ i said/ my mama knows i'm black &
my daddy/ damn sure knows i'm black/ & he is the only one who has a
problem thinkin i'm black/ i said so let me play a white girl/ i'm a
classically trained actress & i need the work & i can do it/ he said that
wdnt be very ethical of him. can you imagine that shit/ not ethical

*natalie*

as a red-blooded white woman/ i cant allow you all to go on like that

*(natalie starts jocularly)*

cuz today i'm gonna be a white girl/ i'll retroactively wake myself up/ ah
low & behold/ a white girl in my bed/ but first i'll haveta call a white girl i
know to have some more accurate information/ what's the first thing white
girls think in the morning/ do they get up being glad they aint niggahs/ do
they remember mama/ or worry abt gettin to work/ do they work?/ do they
play isadora & wrap themselves in sheets & go tip toeing to the kitchen to
make maxwell house coffee/ oh i know/ the first thing a white girl does in
the morning is fling her hair/

so now i'm done with that/ i'm gonna water my plants/ but am i a po
white trash white girl with a old jellyjar/ or am i a sophisticated &
protestant suburbanite with 2 valiums slugged awready & a porcelain
water carrier leading me up the stairs strewn with heads of dolls & nasty
smellin white husband person's underwear/ if i was really protected from
the niggahs/ i might go to early morning mass & pick up a tomato pie on
the way home/ so i cd eat it during the young & the restless. in williams
arizona as a white girl/ i cd push the navaho women outta my way in the
supermarket & push my nose in the air so i wdnt haveta smell them.
coming from bay ridge on the train i cd smile at all the black & puerto
rican people/ & hope they cant tell i want them to go back where they
came from/ or at least be invisible

i'm still in my kitchen/ so i guess i'll just have to fling my hair again

47/

& sit down. i shd pinch my cheeks to bring the color back/ i wonder why
the colored lady hasnt arrived to clean my house yet/ so i cd go to the
beauty parlor & sit under a sunlamp to get some more color back/ it's
terrible how god gave those colored women such clear complexions/ it
take em years to develop wrinkles/ but beauty can be bought & flattered
into the world.

as a white girl on the street/ i can assume since i am a white girl on
the streets/ that everyone notices how beautiful i am/ especially lil black &
caribbean boys/ they love to look at me/ i'm exotic/ no one in their
families looks like me/ poor things. if i waz one of those white girls who
loves one of those grown black fellas/ i cd say with my eyes wide open/
totally sincere/ oh i didnt know that/ i cd say i didnt know/ i cant/ i dont
know how/ cuz i'ma white girl & i dont have to do much of anything.

all of this is the fault of the white man's sexism/ oh how i loathe
tight-assed thin-lipped pink white men/ even the football players lack a
certain relaxed virility. that's why my heroes are either just like my father/
who while he still cdnt speak english knew enough to tell me how the
niggers shd go back where they came from/ or my heroes are psychotic
faggots who are white/ or else they are/ oh/ you know/ colored men.

being a white girl by dint of my will/ is much more complicated than
i thought it wd be/ but i wanted to try it cuz so many men like white girls/
white men/ black men/ latin men/ jewish men/ asians/ everybody. so i
thought if i waz a white girl for a day i might understand this better/ after
all gertrude stein wanted to know abt the black women/ alice adams wrote
*thinking abt billie*/ joyce carol oates has three different black characters
all with the same name/ i guess cuz we are underdeveloped individuals or
cuz we are all the same/ at any rate i'm gonna call this thinkin abt white
girls/ cuz helmut newton's awready gotta book called *white women*/ see
what i mean/ that's a best seller/ one store i passed/ hadda sign said/

> WHITE WOMEN
> SOLD OUT

it's this kinda pressure that forces us white girls to be so absolutely
pathological abt the other women in the world/ who now that they're not
all servants or peasants want to be considered beautiful too. we simply
krinkle our hair/ learn to dance the woogie dances/ slant our eyes with
make-up or surgery/ learn spanish & claim argentinian background/ or as a
real trump card/ show up looking like a real white girl. you know all
western civilization depends on us/

i still havent left my house. i think i'll fling my hair once more/ but
this time with a pout/ cuz i think i havent been fair to the sisterhood/

women's movement faction of white girls/ although/ they always ask what do you people really want. as if the colored woman of the world were a strange sort of neutered workhorse/ which isnt too far from reality/ since i'm still waiting for my cleaning lady & the lady who takes care of my children & the lady who caters my parties & the lady who accepts quarters at the bathroom in sardi's. those poor creatures shd be sterilized/ no one shd have to live such a life. cd you hand me a towel/ thank-you caroline. i've left all of maxime's last winter clothes in a pile for you by the back door. they have to be cleaned but i hope yr girls can make gd use of them.

oh/ i'm still not being fair/ all the white women in the world dont wake up being glad they aint niggahs/ only some of them/ the ones who dont/ wake up thinking how can i survive another day of this culturally condoned incompetence. i know i'll play a tenor horn & tell all the colored artists i meet/ that now i'm just like them/ i'm colored i'll say cuz i have a struggle too. or i cd punish this white beleagered body of mine with the advances of a thousand ebony bodies/ all built like franco harris or peter tosh/ a thousand of them may take me & do what they want/ cuz i'm so sorry/ yes i'm so sorry they were born niggahs. but then if i cant punish myself to death for being white/ i certainly cant in good conscience keep waiting for the cleaning lady/ & everytime i attempt even the smallest venture into the world someone comes to help me/ like if i do anything/ anything at all i'm extending myself as a white girl/ cuz part of being a white girl is being absent/ like those women who are just with a man but whose names the black people never remember/ they just say oh yeah his white girl waz with him/ or a white girl got beat & killed today/ why someone will say/ cuz some niggah told her to give him her money & she said no/ cuz she thought he realized that she waz a white girl/ & he did know but he didnt care/ so he killed her & took the money/ but the cops knew she waz a white girl & cdnt be killed by a niggah especially/ when she had awready said no. the niggah was sposed to hop round the corner backwards/ you dig/ so the cops/ found the culprit within 24 hours/ cuz just like emmett till/ niggahs do not kill white girls.

i'm still in my house/ having flung my hair-do for the last time/ what with having to take 20 valium a day/ to consider the ERA/ & all the men in the world/ & my ignorance of the world/ it is overwhelming. i'm so glad i'm colored. boy i cd wake up in the morning & think abt anything. i can remember emmett till & not haveta smile at anybody.

*maxine (compelled to speak by natalie's pain)*
whenever these things happened to me/ & i waz young/ i wd eat a lot/ or buy new fancy underwear with rhinestones & lace/ or go to the movies/ maybe call a friend/ talk to made-up boyfriends til dawn. this waz when i waz under my parents' roof/ & trees that grew into my room had to be cut back once a year/ this waz when the birds sometimes flew thru the halls

of the house as if the ceilings were sky & i/ simply another winged creature. yet no one around me noticed me especially. no one around saw anything but a precocious brown girl with peculiar ideas. like during the polio epidemic/ i wanted to have a celebration/ which nobody cd understand since iron lungs & not going swimming waznt nothing to celebrate. but i explained that i waz celebrating the bounty of the lord/ which more people didnt understand/ til i went on to say that/ it waz obvious that god had protected the colored folks from polio/ nobody understood that. i did/ if god had made colored people susceptible to polio/ then we wd be on the pictures & the television with the white children. i knew only white folks cd get that particular disease/ & i celebrated. that's how come i always commemorated anything that affected me or the colored people. according to my history of the colored race/ not enough attention was paid to small victories or small personal defeats of the colored. i celebrated the colored trolley driver/ the colored basketball team/ the colored blues singer/ & the colored light heavy weight champion of the world. then too/ i had a baptist child's version of high mass for the slaves in new orleans whom i had read abt/ & i tried to grow watermelons & rice for the dead slaves from the east. as a child i took on the burden of easing the ghost-colored-folks' souls & trying hard to keep up with the affairs of my own colored world.

when i became a woman, my world got smaller. my grandma closed up the windows/ so the birds wdnt fly in the house any more. waz bad luck for a girl so yng & in my condition to have the shadows of flying creatures over my head. i didnt celebrate the trolley driver anymore/ cuz he might know i waz in this condition. i didnt celebrate the basketball team anymore/ cuz they were yng & handsome/ & yng & handsome cd mean trouble. but trouble waz when white kids called you names or beat you up cuz you had no older brother/ trouble waz when someone died/ or the tornado hit yr house/ now trouble meant something abt yng & handsome/ & white or colored. if he waz yng & handsome that meant trouble. seemed like every one who didnt have this condition/ so birds cdnt fly over yr head/ waz trouble. as i understood it/ my mama & my grandma were sending me out to be with trouble/ but not to get into trouble. the yng & handsome cd dance with me & call for sunday supper/ the yng & handsome cd write my name on their notebooks/ cd carry my ribbons on the field for gd luck/ the uncles cd hug me & chat for hours abt my growing up/ so i counted all 492 times this condition wd make me victim to this trouble/ before i wd be immune to it/ the way colored folks were immune to polio.

i had discovered innumerable manifestations of trouble: jealousy/ fear/ indignation & recurring fits of vulnerability that lead me right back to the contradiction i had never understood/ even as a child/ how half the world's population cd be bad news/ be yng & handsome/ & later/ eligible & interested/ & trouble.

plus/ according to my own version of the history of the colored people/ only white people hurt little colored girls or grown colored women/ my mama told me only white people had social disease & molested children/ and my grandma told me only white people committed unnatural acts. that's how come i knew only white folks got polio/ muscular dystrophy/ sclerosis/ & mental illness/ this waz all verified by the television. but i found out that the colored folks knew abt the same vicious & disease-ridden passions that the white folks knew.

the pain i succumbed to each time a colored person did something that i believed only white people did waz staggering. my entire life seems to be worthless/ if my own folks arent better than white folks/ then surely the sagas of slavery & the jim crow hadnt convinced anyone that we were better than them. i commenced to buying pieces of gold/ 14 carat/ 24 carat/ 18 carat gold/ every time some black person did something that waz beneath him as a black person & more like a white person. i bought gold cuz it came from the earth/ & more than likely it came from south africa/ where the black people are humiliated & oppressed like in slavery. i wear all these things at once/ to remind the black people that it cost a lot for us to be here/ our value/ can be known instinctively/ but since so many black people are having a hard time not being like white folks/ i wear these gold pieces to protest their ignorance/ their disconnect from history. i buy gold with a vengeance/ each time someone appropriates my space or my time without permission/ each time someone is discourteous or actually cruel to me/ if my mind is not respected/ my body toyed with/ i buy gold/ & weep. i weep as i fix the chains round my neck/ my wrists/ my ankles. i weep cuz all my childhood ceremonies for the ghost-slaves have been in vain. colored people can get polio & mental illness. slavery is not unfamiliar to me. no one on this planet knows/ what i know abt gold/ abt anything hard to get & beautiful/ anything lasting/ wrought from pain. no one understands that surviving the impossible is sposed to accentuate the positive aspects of a people.

(alec is the only member of the company able to come immediately to maxine. when he reaches her, lou, in his full magician's regalia, freezes the whole company)

lou
yes yes yes      3 wishes is all you get
   scarlet ribbons for yr hair
   a farm in mississippi
   someone to love you madly
all things are possible

but aint no colored magician in his right mind
gonna make you white
cuz this is blk magic you lookin at
& i'm fixin you up good/ fixin you up good & colored
& you gonna be colored all yr life
& you gonna love it/ bein colored/ all yr life
colored & love it/ love it/ bein colored

> (lou beckons the others to join him in the chant, "colored & love it." it becomes a
> serious celebration, like church/ like home/ but then lou freezes them suddenly.)

lou
crackers are born with the right to be
alive/ i'm making ours up right here
in yr face/ & we gonna be
colored & love it

> (the huge minstrel mask comes down as company continues to sing "colored & love it/
> love it being colored." blackout/ but the minstrel mask remains visible. the company
> is singing "colored & love it being colored" as audience exits)

# a photograph:
## lovers in motion

C A S T

*sean david*   photographer

*michael*   dancer

*nevada*   attorney

*claire*   model

*earl*   attorney


*A Photograph* was presented by Joseph Papp's New York Shakespeare Festival under the title: *A Photograph: A Still Life With Shadows/ A Photograph: A Study in Cruelty*, in 1977, with the following personnel:

*Oz Scott*, Director. *Marsha Blanc*, Choreographer. *David Murray*, Composer. *Beverly Parks*, Costume Design. *Victor En Yu Tan*, Lighting. *David Mitchell*, Scenery. *Collis Davis* and *David Mitchell*, Visuals. With: *Avery Brooks, Count Stovall, Hattie Winston, Michele Shay*, and *Petronia Paley*.

In its present form, *A Photograph: Lovers in Motion* was produced by the Equinox Theatre in Houston, Texas, in 1979, with the following personnel:

*Ntozake Shange*, Director. *Paula Moss*, Choreographer. *David Murray*, Composer of Original Music. *McArthur Binion*, Costume Design. *Bruce Bowen*, Lighting. *John Bos*, Scenery. With: *Avery Brooks, Judye Brandt, Christopher Wycliff, Robbie Moore Wyatt*, and *Nikita Flannel*.

here is an old san francisco flat. rounded corners/ arches/ one large room with darkroom on right side/ in middle of room a luxurious antique sofa/ coffee table/ plants/ to right rear/ is a window/ huge with a fire escape/ can see Bay Bridge & some projects/ to the right of desk is a marvelous brass bed/ & rows & rows of books in carefully arranged grocer's boxes. there are photographs/ framed & loose/ copies & originals of diane arbus/ collis davis/ maldonado/ adams/ stieglitz/ van der zee, etc./ an enormous collection of music/ mirrors/ large ones wherever there is space/ to the left of the stage is a door to the flat covered with milky portraits of women carelessly tacked to it. there are carpets & pieces of sculpture/ placed exquisitely. this room has elegance from bein carefully scavenged/ nothin is new. no one knocks because sean never closes the door when he is there.

another area/ used by all characters except sean and michael/ is a plain black space. this area becomes wherever & whatever earl, claire & nevada need it to be.

# A C T  I

## S C E N E  I

*(the set is blacked out so that the lights may create illusions of buildings in the background/ michael is in foreground reviewing a dance with very tiny movements. hear the clicking of a camera that becomes louder & louder. sean enters as d'artagnan is taking michael's picture. she becomes more animated & dances fully. sean keeps taking her picture/ then michael runs into what will be revealed as the bedroom. sean looks about for where she has disappeared to very casually. lights gradually come up. sean at his desk. michael at the bed. sean is in jeans. michael in his shirt & her panties, at the beginning, they were both in street clothes.)*

   *sean (enthusiastically)*
those guys/ frank stewart & pinterhughes/ adger cowan/ they're from new york. & they have never seen what i see/ how cd they? there's no light anywhere like here in san francisco. wait til i get my first show/ there have never been any photographs like the ones i'm gonna take

   *michael (taking a book from the shelves, crosses to stool)*
hey wait/ you're going too fast/ i really want to see what yr talking abt

   *sean*
have you got the cartier-bresson or the dorothea lange? are you really looking/ i mean seeing/ or just turning pages?

*michael*
i'm not just turning pages/ i'm feeling these photographs like i feel dance/
you know/ so a spark gets in my chest/ leaps thru my calves & thighs til i
wanna jump up & down

*sean*
if these make you wanna do all that/ wait til you see my pictures/ i'm
gonna have you absolutely beside yrself

*michael*
in a new world/ huh

*sean*
yeah, a new world/ our world

(sean & michael kiss/ earl nudges the door open)

*sean*
hey man/ good to see you/ what's goin on

*earl*
hey sean/ i thought i wd come on by/ i gotta talk to you

*sean*
earl/ this is michael. she's an incredible dancer/ why pretty soon/ she'll be
as good a dancer as i am a photographer

*michael*
don't pay him any mind/ earl. how are you doin

*earl*
not so hot/ actually

*michael*
well sit down & relax. i'll get you a drink

*earl*
sean/ yr really serious abt this photography stuff/ huh

*sean*
earl/ how many times do i have to tell you/ it is not stuff/ i am an artist/
committed to my art

*earl*

it's just i dont understand/ i mean you were poor all yr life/ why you
wanna be a poor starving artist

*sean*

what are you worried abt/ mr. attorney/ i'm a struggling artist/ not a
starving artist/ there's a big difference

*michael*

that's right/ we are struggling artists together/ right sean? we're gonna be
together forever and ever/ and ever

*earl*

so you'll both be at nevada's grand affair this evening then

*michael (to sean)*

oh/ i didnt know we were sposed to go out tonite

*sean*

no. we're not. i have to go myself/ but you won't have to be bothered/ you
wdnt have any fun

*michael*

i wdnt mind/ i'd love to go

*sean*

i said no/ that's that . . . awright

*michael*

i'll go where i please/ awright?

*(michael exits to bedroom)*

i thought it wd be awright/ i'll be there in a minute

*earl*

damn sean/ i didn't mean to start anything

*sean*

forget it man/ it's nothing

*earl*

good. cuz i really wanted to tell somebody

*sean*
you wanted to tell me

*earl*
yeah you/ i cut claire loose

*sean (smiles)*
why you wanna tell me that

*earl*
cuz ever since she found out she cd be a model she aint been the same/ i
cant keep up with her anymore/ not that i really want to/ how she's been
acting/ it's not my thing man

*sean*
aw earl/ give her a chance/ she's just testing you/ that's all. wants to see if
you can stand some competition

*earl (looking at photos of claire)*
how did you get her to do that/ pour jack daniels all over herself/ & get
out the tub at the same time/ smiling/ how she does/ you know . . .

*sean*
it's art. art man. you want this one

*earl*
yeah.

*sean*
you know/ claire's very imaginative

*earl*
well i'ma get on my way

*(michael has entered/ she sees the photograph)*

*michael*
you leaving/ oh which one did sean give you?

*(she takes photo)*

who is that?

*sean*
earl's friend/ claire. i did her portrait for him

(michael puts photo in her bag)

*earl (indignant)*
sean/ i'ma see yr ass tonite at nevada's/awright

*sean*
don't count on it

*earl*
michael/ you take real good care of yrself

*michael*
i'll be fine

(earl exits. michael begins gathering her things)

i'm going now too. i have a rehearsal

*sean*
awright baby/ sorry you gotta go so soon

*michael*
i dont/ i just dont like all the things i waz feeling while earl waz here

*sean*
don't worry abt anything earl says

*michael*
it waznt what earl said/ it waz you/ you the one said i cdnt go to that party/ & that woman's not earl's friend/ judging from those poses

*sean*
michael/ yr special & i think you can understand what i'm about to tell you

(sean gently leads michael to a stool & sits her down)

there are a number of women in my life/ who i plan to keep in my life/ & i'll never let any of them come between us/ between what we have in our world/ you hear.

61/

*(he caresses her)*

you know alexandre dumas waz a clerk
who wrote at night & dreamed of joinin victor hugo's salon
his son/ alexandre dumas/ came by him accidentally
a seamstress with clean firm hands loved him very much.
i'm gonna be the alexandre dumas of my time/ both the father
and the son. alexandre dumas waz a rogue
witta gold watch & a emerald chain
his son hid from him neath the seamstress' bed
the child alexandre fought to stay in the dark
in the small space beneath.
his father's territories included the beds of paris
& the stage/ women who turned heads with honeysuckle voices
& skirts lifted to the hips/ not the constancy of their labor
not the love of their sons.
alexandre dumas sent his son away from him/
hurried to be famous/ his son waited til the moment waz right
& presented his father/ alexandre dumas/ with a man.
alexandre dumas guarded by a legion of fearless free-wheeling
honorable souls/ the count of monte cristo/
d'artagnan/ the man in the iron mask/
were no match for the yng man/ tendin his father.
he sent his son away from him/ thot abt the velvets he wd wear
on the champs-elysées/ alexandre dumas waz the man
who fathered his father as a child/ waz a man who waz lost/
waz a man loved in spite of his beauties.
alexandre dumas tore his son from his mother's
linen & sent his son away from him.
the threat of his own blood too much.
he sent his son to the forest to learn to disappear
but sons come back/ sons come back from where they are forgotten/
these photographs are for them/ they are gonna see our faces/
the visage of the sons/ the sons who wdnt disappear
niggahs who are still alive
i'm gonna go ona rampage/ a raid on the sleeping settlers
this camera's gonna get em

*(sean takes photo of michael)*

   *michael*
i gotta hero you never even heard of

*(sean takes another photo)*

all i know is his name is james or jim/ shortened/
somebody very black & tall/ sophisticated for that time
'fore the war/ & he waznt born here either
born in paris & carried to detroit when he waz five
a french speakin niggah in detroit/ say 1926
& he waz intense
a rich colored boy in the Depression/ a pouter/ a brooder
who took a wife/ who didnt like just men in oooh/ maybe 1943
he hadda boat floatin in the detroit river
served in korea/ gotta be a physician/ did abortions
for girls bout my age when i waz in high school.
i know he owned bars & up from transient hotels
he dealt smack & never hadda son/ i always wanted to meet him.
my daddy & his girl rode in the backseat of the newest
& hottest car in nashville/ on the way to where
fletcher henderson might be/ some all colored spot
& he/ jim wd buy lotsa whiskey/ & listen
seem to be treating daddy & his girl/ who waz poor
but they were working making sure jim didnt kill anyone
thinking he waz some mad music. another kinda miles davis/
an assassin of his own love. so on the way back from anywhere
my daddy & his girl rode in the front/ jim lay molten on the back.
& he wd stay in his room til his parents left campus or
til his wife's lover left town.
everybody knew abt her/ that she liked to touch women's legs
& mouths/ that there waz nothing cd be done
cuz she had connections/ & he waz so sharp & he took her
& the sorority took her/ & there waz nothing cd be done
cuz she waz beautiful. & then there he waz & wd you mess
wit him who is anger/ a malignant fury in his glance
when somebody wanted to say/ what everybody knew abt her
& they did leave him alone. & how cd he not know
& if he did know/ it must be/ he really is a foreigner
not a whole man himself/ to have a woman so
a woman so fulla beauty/ she shared when a breeze fell
from her hands/ & he never left her.
i waited & waited to meet him
& i've just found out how i waz in love wit this man
who has died/ & i never knew him to touch
i never even saw a picture/ but not far from me
never far from me/ i've kept a lover
who waznt all-american/ who didnt believe/ wdnt straighten up.
oh i've loved him in my own men/ sometimes hateful
sometimes subtle like high fog & sun/ but who i loved

63/

is yr not believing. i loved yr bitterness & hankered
after that space in you where you are outta control/
where you cannot touch or you wd kill me/ or somebody else
who loved you. i never even saw a picture
& i've loved him all my life
he is all my insanity
& anyone who loves me wd understand

(michael exits. lights fade)

## S C E N E   I I

(sean at his desk with a camera, claire in scarlet camisole & lace panties
is dancing sensuously, posing, with intentions of making love)

claire
ooohhh . . . take my picture daddy

sean
that's what i'm here for

claire (on bed)
how's this? how's this? i dont want to take anymore pictures. i
think i might be coming down wit something

sean
well. i'm not

claire
coming down/ or with something?

sean
do you value yr life?

claire
maybe it's just the way i smell today/ i dont smell like you at all/
see/ these aint yours/ & this neither/ i know/ i know/ i smell like
andrew/ no/ charlie/ oh that cdnt be/ i dont know anybody
named charlie . . . i know/ i smell like willie/ wondrous willie

sean
cant leave willie alone can ya/ say you coming down with
something/ & cant talk bout nothing but how willie smells

*claire*
i gotta . . . i gotta tell you something

*sean*
huh

*claire*
i got rhinestones up there now/ did ya know that

*sean*
no/ uh huh i didnt

*claire*
yeah. rhinestones & palm leaves & a great big ol magnolia

*sean*
willie put alla that up there

*claire*
no. now let me see. who waz it/ i mighta forgot somebody john/ no/
andrew/ no . . . oh i know who gave claire all these treasures/ waz claire. i
waz planning on being the sea & bein swept over by some pirates/ ya
know/ carried on a rakish sea captain's back/ into a lagoon/ ya gonna be a
pirate sean/ i gotta treasure up in there/ a magic magnolia

*sean*
say you coming down with something/ something from willie

*claire*
oh/ yr being too serious/ willie's just a sweet friend

*sean*
willie aint been straight since NAM/ & willie aint the only one neither.
there's andrew/ & charlie/ & james

*claire*
no. you are the only one/ c'mon you got it/ mama's got it all for you/ a fine
magnolia wrapped in rhinestones/ c'mon it's right here/ i waz only teasing

*sean*
c'mere claire/ i got something for ya. if you ever so much as look at willie/
or come down with something/ i'm gonna take you down to the 500 club
on fillmore/ & give everybody some of that magnolia . . .

65 /

*(sean forces whiskey into claire's mouth)*

. . . understand

   *claire (backs up wiping her face)*
i dont need you for that/ sean. i can do that by myself. but you can come
watch/ if you wanna

   *sean*
you gonna watch something/ you gonna watch me/ get alla them
rhinestones/ palm leaves & every petal of magnolia

   *(sean picks claire up/ tumbles onto bed with her)*

   *claire*
oooohh . . . come to mama . . .

   *sean*
you know what alexandre dumas wrote abt his mama/ claire?

   *claire*
no . . . i dont know nothing abt that. why do i have to think abt that now

   *sean*
the only crime for which i will never forgive myself is to have doubted
my mother. aint that heavy?

   *claire*
yeah, it's heavy

   *(sean gets up)*

ooooh sean . . .

   *sean*
ooohh michael

   *claire*
who the fuck is michael?

   *sean (crossing to claire)*
you say you got palm leaves up in there?

   *(lights out)*

# SCENE III

*(lights up immediately on nevada & earl, in formal evening dress, at a party at nevada's house)*

nevada
earl/ do you see that/ i cant believe anyone is still wearing costume jewelry/ especially at my party

earl
not everyone can afford real gold/ nevada

nevada
then they shdnt wear anything

earl
that's an option . . .

nevada
i wonder when sean's going to get here

earl
he told me he waz studying "the count of monte cristo" by dumas

nevada
the count of monte cristo/ sean knows quite enuf abt swashbuckling awready

earl
he needs what you & i have/ nevada. he needs some sense of his future. that a black man lived to hear his name shouted in the streets

nevada
but dumas waz so common/ earl

earl
he waz a man of letters/ and passion

nevada
alexandre dumas waz the same as these wild niggah artists are today

earl
dont try to rein him in too much/ nevada. he's gotta be free

*nevada*

he shd come here/ i cd tell him how dumas' bastard son felt abt his
father's freedom.

*(low light up on sean in bed with claire)*

*sean*

alexandre dumas took to women/ adulation/ scandal & wine

*(light down on sean)*

*nevada*

you wanted sean to know that/ earl

*earl*

yeah. see whatta niggah cd do when the rest of us were slaves

*nevada*

no/ no. YOU all were slaves/ i keep telling you that/ earl. you remember
the nite i passed my bar exam/ & we all three got drunk & went to the
sapphire room/ & i danced on the bar & put on one of the other girls' wigs/
& you & sean were so happy. i cd see you/ letting me go/ letting me be
wild/ & i want to give him some part of me like in the bar . . . wd you get
sean/ earl/ wd you . . .

*(lights fade)*

# S C E N E   I V

*(sean & michael in bed)*

*sean*

i really like the way you look/ sleepin like that/ yr face in the mornin/ is a
blessin/ some women/ i look at them/ i wanna get up . . . but you/ i wanna
go back to the womb with you

*michael*

sean/ somebody's been sleeping here recently/ just like me

*sean*

you know somebodies have been sleeping here/ & you know yr here now
& that is all you need to know . . . damn/ you are so soft . . .

*michael*
no/ it's important/ i cant lay in any old body's morning & evening smells/ i
want an arrangement for me/ i know/ when i'm here i'll bring my japanese
mats & we can sleep on the floor

*sean (laughing)*
you mean yr not upset abt them bein here/ just bout where you sleep?

*michael*
uh huh

*sean*
well/ i'll be damned. what kinda woman are ya/ dont you wanna know/
why i need somebody else sides you/ & where am i going & who is that/
how much do i love you & all that stuff?

*michael*
no

*sean*
well/ i dont know how long this is gonna last/ but it sure feels funny

*michael*
feels funny?

*sean*
dont be getting all holy & above possession/ aint a bitch in the world cant
get jealous & loud/ they been running me crazy

*michael*
that's them

*(she begins push-ups)*

i cant do that. i'm physically incapable of chasing & arguing abt a man/ i
just cant. i dont have the energy

*sean*
awright/ but i'm not gonna hold you to any of this/ i think yr just feeling
well taken care of . . . my ladies are genuinely wild/ & feline/ they're not
gonna like this very much

69/

*michael*
they're not gonna like what

*sean*
you n me together/ see like lovers in bed/ come on/ michael

*michael*
oh/ i'm not gonna be that way/ you'll see. i work hard as you to make my art take up the slack for my life

*sean*
you know/ alexandre dumas had a thing for dancers/ too

*michael*
i didnt know claire waz a dancer

*sean*
oh yeah?

*michael (crossing to bed)*
oh yeah

*sean*
oh yeah?

*michael*
oh yeah . . . i won't make any trouble at all/ sean. i wont make any trouble at all.

*(lights fade)*

## SCENE V

*(earl & claire, at earl's office)*

*claire*
alexandre dumas waz still a niggah/ sean must know that alla those fancy waistcoats/ 2 bastards/ a boy & a girl by two different women/ he had women all over paris/ hanging out wit the fellas/ victor hugo/ alfred de vigny/ alla them still thot he was a niggah. some actress usedta have all the house windows opened in the theater cuz when alexandre dumas showed up/ when he showd up she claimed she smelled an acrid stench/ the stench of a niggah. sean smells like a niggah/ maybe i'll tell him he smells like alexandre dumas

*earl*
you shd do that/ claire

*claire*
you gotta nerve saying what i shd & shdnt do. the little time i spent wit you/ if i tried to kiss you/ you got scared.

*earl*
claire/ that's not why i left you

*claire*
then tell me why you never loved me like i wanted

*earl*
because i respect myself/ that's why

*claire*
well earl/ you smell like a niggah too/ if you sweat. do you sweat/ earl?

*earl*
don't you remember

*claire*
have you ever sweat/ earl?

*earl*
til the bed's wringing wet

*claire (pauses)*
i'd rather talk this kinda talk to sean

*earl*
suit yrself

(lights out)

S C E N E  VI

(michael choreographing a dance in sean's studio. claire enters)

*michael (responding to her movement & music)*
that's it . . .

*claire*
hey hey hey/ if it isnt michael. it is michael/ isnt it?

71/

michael
yes it is/ & yr claire for sure

claire
yep/ the one & only/ where's sean

michael
i think he went out . . . yes/ he's out/ you wanna wait?

claire
i dont need an invitation from you

(michael resumes dance/ claire watches from sean's desk)

i need some entertainment. i'm bored. why dontchu entertain me/ yr a
dancer/ do a dance/ for me

michael
i am doing a dance/ & you can watch/ but it's not entertainment

claire (crosses to bed, takes off shoes & takes out some cocaine)
you artists are so damn serious/ dont you ever have fun?

michael (seeing the coke, she gets a glass of whiskey for claire)
here claire/ i'm sorry to have been so inhospitable

(michael takes cocaine snorter from claire, crosses room & leans on sean's desk)

claire (facetiously)
you want some?

michael
i wd really like you to relax around me/ claire

claire
i want to relax around sean

michael
thats what i mean/ claire. you dont haveta stay all nervous & fidgety til he
gets here. i cd give you a massage

claire
dont you bother. i'll get plenty muscle relaxation when sean gets here

*michael*

you really like him dont you/ you like the way he touches you/ huh?

*claire*

oh yes. he touches me somewhere & i cd feel him all over

*michael*

i cd make you feel like that even when sean's not here/ when he's
working or sleeping/ there's a technique i learned in dance/ that'll really
help

*claire*

is it fun?

*michael (crossing to bed)*

oh yes/ it's a lot of fun. so relax yr whole body & let yr breath flow even &
slow/ just as if sean waz with you/

*(she massages claire)*

is this how sean makes you feel?

*claire*

not quite/ why you keep talking about sean? oh stop . . . yr hurting me!

*(sean enters from bedroom/ groggy/ grasps situation & crosses to bed. michael realizes
he is in the room, but holds claire to the bed forcibly)*

*sean*

claire/ what the fuck are you doin/ michael/ get the hell up offa her

*claire (struggling to get out of michael's grip)*

i thot you were out

*sean*

yeah/ i bet you thot i waz out/ so you cd get michael involved in yr sick
shit/ get the hell outta here

*michael*

sean/ there is nothing wrong/ i waz just giving claire a massage

*sean*

whatchu need a massage for/ claire/ whatchu coming over here to get a
massage for

73 /

*michael (still sneaking some of claire's cocaine)*
sean/ what's wrong with you? i gave claire a massage/ & that's all


    *sean (trying to get claire off bed and out)*
damn. i cant trust you to stay outta trouble for a minute. claire/ you set
this up. you were probably bored/ is that it claire/ were you bored/ so you
thot it wd be good to play with michael/ get outta here/ no/ dont put on yr
shoes/ carry them/ just get out


    *claire*
keep yr hands offa me


    *(to michael, who has her cocaine snorter)*

give me that/ michael


    *(michael smiles, returns snorter)*


    *sean*
shut up & get out/ go away right now/ & think of something else to do wit
yrself/ just get the hell out


    *(claire exits, sean crosses down stage right to michael, who is sitting on her stool)*

michael/ just what the fuck waz that all abt?


    *michael*
i told you/ nothing. i just gave the girl a massage


    *sean (grabs her arm)*
well/ why were you laying all over the girl/ just to give the girl a massage


    *michael*
i told you/ nothing


    *sean*
anything else you wanna tell me


    *michael (breaking away)*
no. yr hurtin my arm/ i dont like it when you hurt me. that's all i have to
say

sean *(reluctantly apologetic)*
i'm sorry michael/ it waznt yr fault/ it waz that simple perverted bitch . . .

*(sean caresses michael, who is smiling innocently. lights out.)*

## S C E N E  VII

*(claire, in her bedroom)*

claire
be soft & brown/ be slick & claire
remember who covers yr back/ yr backside
is coverin yr back/ miz claire
yr body is the blood & the flesh
god gave his only daughter/ to save alla his sons
daddy waz right/ daddy waz absolutely right/
give a man exactly what he wants & he wants you/
simple as that. but what about claire
claire wants a present
a lil jack daniels/ a lil blow

*(claire slugs some whiskey/ rubs coke on her gums)*

i know what feels good/ tender
like the inside of my thigh
but i dont know anybody who wd give claire a lil
just a lil
i'm just too good feeling
for such a simple lil thing
i'm just too good feeling
for such a simple lil thing

*(lights fade on claire)*

## S C E N E  VIII

*(lights up on sean & michael in same position as we left them)*

sean
michael      michael      michael/ sweet lil michael/ smart lil michael/ can
i take yr picture/ now i wanna lick yr face/ i wanna lick yr lips yr
everywhere/ hey smartass/ michael come over here. i want you to see
something

*(sean gets remote control slide changer/ brings michael next to him. light flashes indicates slides)*

look at this/ here's a woman/ she's a muslim

michael
she's a muslim/ well/ how cd you know that?

sean
i watched her every morning/ she lives cross the street on the 7th floor/ she gets up at 6:15/ everyday/ she must cuz she's in the shower by 6:20/ sometimes i cant get to sleep for thinking bout her in the shower with the water coatin her skin/ she smells like magnolia . . .

michael
how do you know?

sean
she shops round the open market like i do/ i even tip my hat to her old man/ when i see him/ & then i think bout how he cdnt imagine how much pleasure she gives me . . .

michael *(joking a lil)*
that's horrible/ sean. yr no better than a peeping tom

*(light flashes for another slide)*

oh no . . .

sean
what do you mean "oh no." these niggahs mean business. you see what they did to that dummy/ dont you/ knocked her plaster ass right down on the ground/ yes they did. & just cuz they felt like it.

michael
i suppose that means something to you. besides they are vicious/ they wda loved to hit a living woman/ sean/ dont you see/ they were wishing that mannequin waz a real body to break.

sean
yeah. yr absolutely right & i've got it all there in that frame. i gotta whole dynamic of centuries/ in a two-dimensional plane/ i'm telling you michael/ stick with me/ i'm a genius for unravelling the mysteries of the

darker races/ sometimes our spit seems to be brine from the sea & those
ships/ a grease burn on some woman looks like a brand/ michael/ i swear i
know who we are . . . i know who we are

   *michael*
there's more . . . there's gotta be more/ sean

   *sean*
like dance/ right? somethin i cant have or return to/ somethin dim in
memory/ barely articulated

   (*michael begins to dance*)

   *michael*
i am space & winds
like a soft rain or a torrent of dust/ i can move
be free in time/ a moment is mine always
i am not like a flower at all
tho i can bloom & be a wisp of sunlight
i'm a rustling of dead leaves
collections of ol women by the weddin
the legs of a cotton club queen
& so familiar with tears
alla this is mine/ so long as i breathe/ i'm gonna dance
for all of us/ everybody dead/ everybody busy
everybody too burdened to jump thru a nite
a hot & bluesy jump in the guts of ourselves
a dance is like a dream/ i can always remember
make it come again . . . i can make it come again

   *sean (crossing to michael)*
michael/ a photograph is like a fingerprint/ it stays
& stays forever/ we cd have something forever/ just how
we want it. give me a camera & i cd get you anything
you wanted/ breeze/ a wad of money/ madness/ women on
back porches kneading bread/ stars falling/ ice cream
& drunks & forever/ i cd give you forever in a night sky/
michael/ i cd give you love/ pure & full/ in a photograph . . .
when i get these museum shows i'm gonna give you whatever
you want. anything you want.

   (*sean embraces michael/ a horn honks repeatedly*)

michael
sean/ is that anybody for you?

sean
no

*(sean & michael continue to kiss & hug. nevada enters, crosses the room without being noticed by the lovers)*

nevada
so. yr working/ huh. too busy to be bothered with me/ less the rent's due. or you need some film. or yr "model" needs whatever those kinda women need. you dont love me. you never loved me. me/ nevada/ is nothing to you but a few bucks & a easy fuck/ niggah you never took my picture/ you never take my picture/ you dont think i'm beautiful or nothing, just these slut artist bitches/ beautiful women of color/ with good form. an artist/ an ass. that's what i've been messing with/ i cd have had anybody i wanted/ i am not an ordinary nothing/ my family waz manumitted in 1843/ yall were still slaves/ carrying things for white folks/ just slaves/ that's what you come from & i cd do better/

*(nevada rips photographs from walls and desk, tears them to bits.)*

i dont need you or nothing from you do you hear me tramp/ sean do you hear me/ i dont need you/ yr photographs/ yr dick/ nothing/ you've got nothing i want/ i just wanted you to take my picture . . . my picture/ make my face belong to you/ like her/ like that slut who cant talk/ cant you talk bitch/ low down cunt/ if i waz you i'd bury myself

*(michael swings at nevada, sean grabs nevada and pulls her away)*

sean
i dont want yr face/ nevada. i got what i want from you/ you love me dont you? well/ that's all i want/ i'm probably the only real thing in yr life & i can feel it/ how you love me/ but if you want me to take yr picture/ i gotta see something in yr face/ yr love for me in yr face/ ya hear? now let me get back to work.

nevada *(regaining her composure)*
*(to sean)* i'll expect yr call . . . *(to michael)* when you finish yr work.

*(nevada leaves quietly. sean picks up fragments of photos/ is on the verge of rage. michael is rocking catatonically on the stool)*

*sean (holding fragments of photos)*

see michael. lil bits of people/ lil bits of flesh/ living folks. i've got em
right here. i finally got something/ breathing/ this must be that old dude/
looked sorta like my grandpa/ drunk. oh god waz he drunk. stink too. but
his hands/ his hands were like mississippi fields/ his hands were cotton &
blood/ & strong/ that muthafuckah waz strong/ musta been a helluva ladies
man/ wearin the dirtiest cashmere coat i ever saw/ but his hands/ i got
those. damn/ michael dont you understand anything? there. there are the
eyes of the cashier at the porno house & this is niggahs asleep in the park.
what's this. oh this is fog/ but my god i gotta world now/ i gotta world i'm
making in my image/ i got something for a change/ lil sean david who
never got over on nothing but bitches/ is building a world in his image/
YALL GOT THAT? michael/ you gotta understand/ you haveta
understand/ i saw these things/ these people gave me something i love/
things i love . . .

*(low light up on earl)*

*earl*

sean david loves trinkets/ like alexandre dumas showing up at the duc
d'orleans for an audience with the king/ dressed up like a mardi gras
clown. keeping women waiting in the wings/ taking his scenarios from a
vast collection of parisian pussy. yr gonna haveta marry nevada/ say when
dumas married ida ferrier/ he said/ "my dear fellow, it waz the only way
to get rid of her."

*(light out on earl)*

*sean*

nevada is really death/ she gotta be death to do something like this/ that's
why i cant do her portrait

*michael*

sean/ did i ever tell you abt my grandma/ the one who sat on her porch
with a shotgun/ sean. i'm talking to you

*sean*

what are you talking abt

*michael*

my grandma from carolina who got a shotgun to take care of her family
when grandpa waz lynched

*sean*
please michael/ not now

*michael*
if not now when/ when sean? i sat in this room & watched you take all
this shit from some bitch cuz she's got money & you ain't/ cuz you think
being a nigger is being nothing/ bein put upon & taken/ well i'm telling
you i dont come from that/ & i cant watch you be that/ my people took
care of themselves. i am an artist too. i go to work/ in a nasty ol
restaurant/ & you let some woman destroy yr photographs/ well/ my
grandma carried a shotgun/ do you understand me

*sean*
i dont believe you/ i just dont believe you. yr making things up again. it's
not the same for you & me

*michael*
oh yes it is. it's our lives/ our grandparents & their uncles/ it's how we
came to be/ by taking our lives seriously/ we fight for every breath every
goddamn day/ do you know that

*sean*
i wda known if niggahs waz alla what you say/ i wd know abt something
else besides the welfare/ the white folks/ heroin & whores/ darling

*michael*
i'm telling you the truth. I'm telling you my grandma carried a shotgun &
sat on her porch. telling us abt garvey/ du bois/ the colored horse soldiers
& jack johnson

*sean*
michael you got too much/ & you know too goddamn much

*michael*
it's ours. alla ours. dont nobody own history/ cant nobody make ours but
us. & look at what you've done to yrself

*sean*
no. dont look at me/ what i did to myself/ huh/ no. look down on fillmore
at the junkies & little girls selling pussy/ the pawn shops & bars/
specializing in knife fights & chitlins/ some muthafucking history. well/
i'll tell you/ my daddy hadda monkey/ do you hear/ a monkey he treated
better than me

michael
we're alla that. alla the blood & the fields & the satchels dragging in the
dust. all the boogies & stairways late at night oozing the scent of love &
cornbread/ the woods smelling of burnt flesh & hunger

sean
how come nobody ever told me

michael
i'm telling you. my grandma's trying to tell you. she speaks thru me.

sean
shit. fuck yr grandma

(michael is furious/ crosses to get her dance clothes & shawl/ crosses back to sean)

michael
you selfish muthafucker

(michael exits)

sean
grandma/ grandma's telling me . . . huh/ my grandma don't talk . . . my
daddy speaks for her

(apartment lights fade as light comes up on earl as sean's daddy)

earl (daddy)
i wish she wd die/ she's giving me ulcers she dont know where she's at/
dont even know who i am sometimes she thinks i'm papa/ but i'm telling
you i gotta put up this fence/ cuz she tries to run off all the time. if i ever
opened that gate i'd never find her/ i'm saying she drove me to this/
wandering out talking crazy bout/ she wants to go home . . .

sean
shit/ this is her home

earl (daddy)
is as good as her home/ but i cant let her out/ cuz she wont come back/
sooner she dies i'll have some peace/ cuz she's old she's old/ & she falls
down a lot

sean
i peeked in grandma's room/ i smelled urine/ dirty clothes/ the scent of

81/

the old woman's crotch/ she waz bruised & sleeping in her day dress/ her
bed was unmade

   *earl (daddy)*
i tell ya she gotta go sometime/ i gotta have a life of my own/ what more
cd she ask of me . . . shit . . . i'm just her son

   *(light down on earl)*

   *sean*
you didn't see me/ your son. i'm waiting daddy/ just like you/ waiting for
a one man show/ waiting to be seen & touched/ i am waiting to come back
from the forest . . . daddy/ i want that monkey to die

   *(sean gets his portfolio, takes it to his desk. he looks at the photos he's been hiding*
   *from everyone. nevada enters/ sean quickly hides portfolio)*

   *sean (quickly hiding portfolio)*
what the fuck do you want?

   *nevada*
sean/ i'm really sorry bout the mess i made/ but i'm on my way over to the
museum/ and i wanted to know if you still want me to try to get that show
for you

   *sean*
get the hell on away/ wd you

   *nevada*
so/ the greatest photographer in the world is gonna give up an opportunity
for an exhibit

   *sean*
i'll get it myself/ i dont need you to do that

   *nevada*
all by yrself/ yr gonna build yr name with yr own ignorant lil self/ well/ i
tried

   *(nevada crosses as if to leave/ turns back)*

oh. here's the lens you were looking at last week/ it might come in handy

sean
i dont want it/ nevada

nevada
aw sean/ take it/ i want you to have it/ for yr work

sean
OK nevada/ leave it over there somewhere/ just go away

(nevada carefully puts lens on the bed)

nevada
i love you

sean
i know you do. just leave me alone for a while/ awright? just leave/
nevada. i'm gonna tell you one more time. go away.

(nevada looks at lens, then at sean)

nevada
one more time/ huh . . . one more time/ one more lens . . .

(nevada exits. sean goes to bed & puts lens on camera, smilin & enjoying himself.
michael enters quietly/ watches him carefully;

sean (to himself)
i cda promised that bitch anything

michael
for what/ one more lens?

sean
michael/ dont mess wit me

michael
i wont have to/ i'm leaving

sean
good/ i'm not doing portraits this afternoon

michael
will you listen/ i'm not staying anymore

sean
what the hell is this/ a loving gesture?

michael
in a way/ it'll keep me loving myself

sean
i dont play that shit/ michael. when i am working/ i am working/ when
i'm fucking i'm fucking/ & now i am working/ we'll talk abt this later

michael
i'm not going anywhere yet

sean
i dont take no orders from no bitch

(michael has moved to sean's desk, and has found his portfolio)

michael
sean/ these are incredible/ why havent you ever shown these?

sean
michael/ what are you doing? those guys are dead anyway/ that waz a long
time ago/ i am not showing no photographs of muthafuckahs who died in
fronta me/ their heads blown off/ legs coming out their fucking eyes/
michael you are outta yr mind/ you got the nerve to say i'm cold-blooded

michael (looking thru portfolio)
isnt this something to you?

sean (making sexual gestures)
what has fucking & kissing gotta do with my work?

michael
i'm not talking bout what you do with me & nevada & claire

sean
yr crazy

michael
OK/ so i'm crazy. but i know what you are capable of

sean
you dont know a damn thing abt me/ cept i take care of yr never get enuf
ass

*michael*
i cant get enuf if its not real

*sean*
yr really outta yr mind/ stupid bitch/ i know how to deal with you/ or any
other bitch comes in here

*michael*
i thot you were telling me abt yr art/ not how you stay alive

*sean*
i do whatever i haveta to stay alive

*michael*
that's what i mean/ yr not even trying to be an artist/ yr trying to stay alive

*sean*
i thot art waz survival

*michael*
no. it's love. it's fighting to give something/ it's giving yrself to someone/
who loves you

*sean*
give myself?

*michael*
yeah. lettin everybody in & giving up what is most treasured

*sean*
i aint got no treasures

*michael*
then yr not alive

*sean*
well/ you still here. you visit dead folks often?

*michael*
sometimes. sometimes i prove i'm alive by watching em

*sean*
well. i dont haveta do that

*michael*
then let me go

*sean*
you are sucha dumb bitch. if it's not you/ there'll be somebody else

*michael*
forever?

*sean*
long as i'm living

*michael*
what a waste of time

*sean*
waste of time/ say you dont like how i do you?

*michael*
i dont like thinking that you think yr dick means more to me than yr
work/ you dont give yrself anymore than anyone is willing to give you

*sean (grabbing michael)*
nobody gives me nothing

*michael*
i cd give you something

*sean (pulls her down, fighting)*
oh yeah? you come round here to get what i got/ i give it to you & you
give me what you got/ that's what's going on here

*michael*
that's not enuf

*sean*
it's plenty/ i'm living aint i/ i'm not out on the street am i/ i'm not
pimping anybody

*michael*
arent you?

*sean*
you so damn dumb/ i explained all this to you a million times

86/

michael
i thot you were a man

sean
i fuck you fool/ you still dont know i'ma man?

michael
i mean somebody who loves in the world/ loves himself & his work & some people

sean
i told you i'm gonna be the greatest photographer in the world

michael
how abt being the photographer you haveta be

sean (lets her go/ crosses to bed)
you talking nonsense

michael (aggressively follows him)
will you love yrself to keep working/ if the muthafuckahs in washington say yr work aint shit/ if the galleries in northbeach say niggah/ yr work aint shit/ can you love yr photographs/ sean/ if they dont get you what you want?

sean (pushes her down on bed)
no. & wd you leave me the fuck alone

michael
i'm not afraid of you

sean
well/ then get afraid

(sean grabs michael again/ more struggling/ then he lets her go. she moves away/ in pain)

michael
when you work on yr pictures like you worked on me/ i'll believe you/ right now i think yr fulla shit & i'm ashamed cuz i believed you at least loved photography

sean
i do. i do. yr getting everything confused michael. i dont know what yr talking abt/ i do love my pictures

                 *michael*
do you love me?


                 *sean*
why you gonna ask me something like that?


                 *michael*
cuz i wanted to see if you'll ever be honest


                 *sean*
i dont know/ i dont know what yr talking abt/ i wanna say i love you/
michael/ i wanna say it/ but i dont know what yr talking abt/ i wanna
know/ michael/ i wanna tell you something/ but i really dont know


         *(michael crosses toward door/ puts on her shawl to leave/ turns around to sean)*


                 *michael*
you cd try/ say anything . . . anything that's true


         *(lights fade on michael in the background)*


                 *sean*
when you get to be a man/ you can go to the whorehouse
with me/ that's what he usedta say
tho he brought the whores home/ & fucked em
& beat em & fought em & laughed all nite long

lil boy what did you do/ while he fed his monkey?

when you can swim like me/ he said/ you'll be a man
& stuck me in the water with my diapers on.
at dinner time daddy waz asleep/ head on the table
& bottle nearby

lil boy what did you do/ while he fed his monkey?

soft-eyed child with good straight legs
soft-eyed child with wet sheets every nite
i lay there all day til they dried sometimes
to be a man

lil boy silent & making no trouble/ what did you do/
while he fed his monkey?


        *88/*

my daddy didnt like me/ daddy didnt like me
he usedta say/ mama neither but it dont matter
cuz i'm not theirs no how/ i'ma man
i am a man
& he wd cry & drink his vodka/ with the lady whose name
i cdnt know/ cuz i waz running the hallways
looking for a daddy

lil boy lil boy/ niggah tell me
what did you do while he fed his monkey
michael/ what did i do while he fed his monkey . . .
what did i do/ while he fed his monkey

    *michael (moving toward sean but not touching him)*
you just wanted somebody to love you/ that's all
you just wanted somebody to love you

    *(lights fade to black)*

# A C T   I I

## S C E N E   I X

*(nevada & earl, on the porch of sean's rooming house)*

### nevada
go on earl/ if you go talk with him/ he'll listen/ he won't listen to me

### earl
oh really?

### nevada
yes really. he thinks you can handle yrself/ n women like me just make
him mad/ most of the time

### earl
nevada/ you ever think abt yrself sometimes steada sean? i mean
goddamn/ yr a helluva prize/ let him come to terms with you for a change

### nevada
no. i'm scared

### earl
scared?

### nevada
not of sean/ everything. i'm just wound up over myself/ i cant reach out to
anybody/ but i cant let go & i cant hold on & go speak to him/ earl/ i wanta
drink

### earl
you dont need a drink/ nevada/ i guess i just dont know why you gotta do
this

### nevada
i need him/ he lets me breathe or something like i can feel/ i get close & i
haveta have that/ i haveta have that/ that's all i've got

### earl
awright i'll talk to him/ but you need something else

### nevada
no. i dont need nothin else. i gotta office/ i gotta porsche/ i gotta family &

a name/ & i never had nothin for myself/ just this stupidness/ running
around being important/ bein highfaluting/ all this time pushing for what
isnt ever gonna be mine/ i do i do/ need somebody

   *earl*
somebody quiet & concerned & rich & brown & never been mean & wont
be/ really nevada/ sean doesnt know bout much more than women &
cruelty/ i usedta wish i cd be half of what he feels in women/ just a lil less
correct/ but you aint it/ nevada/ you arent ready for what you think you
want

   *nevada*
oh yeah/ i am/ i am as ready as that michael/ that slutty dancer

   *earl*
nevada/ you know yr lovely/ & shd be handled gently

   *nevada*
stop it

   *earl*
awright. awright/ i'm gonna go right up there & get him so you can get off
listening to him tell you to take yr hincty black ass home/ cuz you may
not have anything you want/ but you got everything sean ever dreamed of/
& he cant stand it/ he really cant stand it

   *(earl watches as nevada takes a swig from her flask/ lights fade)*

## SCENE X

   *(michael & sean in bed/ michael begins a ritual dance, like a fairy tale in motion)*

   *michael*
broken boats/ bones & spit/ useless solitary legs/ legs & splintered trees/
winds & sea jumped thru flesh & breath/ twenty men tossed on shore/
some in clothes soppin in seaweed/ others with swollen bleeding bodies/
the storm had thrown them in a strange land/ they were looking for the
silver snake/ they knew the silver snake kept a woman whose kiss wd
make hunger disappear & wounds heal/ the woman who belonged to the
star-lit snake swung her ankle from an acacia tree in the face of the
shipwrecked sailors/ they stood afraid/ the woman's toes rested on the
scarlet tongue of a snake so bright/ the night drew back & ran off with the
sea/ while the star-lit silver snake kisst the corners of her mouth/ daring
the universe to take her

91/

*(michael gets back onto bed with sean)*

oh/ i love it/ making things beautiful. you/ my star-lit silver snake/ do you love it?

   *sean (getting up)*

yes. yes/ but that's too simple. i know/ i'ma tell you one

   *michael*
you gonna tell me one?

   *sean*
yes. that's right. me. i'ma be it. the photographer of all time. look out ansel/ here i am/ ms. arbus/ gordon parks & van derzee/ my name is sean david/ a man from the wild with a lens to capture anything that moves/ anything that sweats/ any shadow breath/ figure or premonition/ yes indeed. i can bring you the world shining grainy focused or shaking/ a godlike phenomenon/ sean david. that'll be $5000 for the first three sittings/ you'll have to see my secretary abt that/ actually/ i'll see my secretary abt seein my tailor/ i realize yr not accustomed to the visions of a man of color who has a gift/ but fear not/ i'll give it to ya a lil at a time. i am only beginning to startle/ to mesmerize & reverse the reality of all who can see. i gotta thing bout niggahs/ my folks/ that just wont stop/ & we are so correct for the photograph/ we profile all the time/ styling/ giving angle & pattern/ shadows & still-life. if somebody sides me cd see the line in niggahs/ the texture of our lives/ they wda done it/ but since nobody has stepped forward/ here i am. yes. sean david. the MOST sensitive MOST conscientious meticulous muthafuckah ever in a darkroom/ oh is that the museums again/ i'll call them back/ i only have 4 assistants/ oh accompany you to paris/ & then to rio? i'll see/ you understand/ of course/ i must go to scandinavia to accept the nobel prize next week/ i think/ next week

   *(sean takes michael's hand/ they stand as if accepting the nobel prize)*

yes. i grew up in the west/ same as dead-eye dick & eric dolphy. i never saw a piece of art/ til i got my first piece of ass/ essie carlton 11½/ & she didnt like to smootch or nothing/ just give it up. i learned to work in the dark like that/ gentlemen/ i've hand-held every photograph in the dark like that/ like essie.

   *(sean crosses quickly/ light flashes for slide)*

look at these lil girls/ michael. aint that something/ see how they're
digging into each other

*michael*
my god sean/ why didnt you stop them

*sean*
no/ michael/ this is more important than stopping that one fight/ look at
the hatred in that child/ she hates another lil girl/ exactly like herself/ this
is a colored childhood michael/ me stopping that one fight wont have
done anything

*michael*
but sean/ they're bleeding

*sean*
yeah. that's the point

*michael*
they're children & you've made them animals

*sean*
but now i'm holding the nobel prize cuz i . . . i cd see niggahs living in
the dark/ & my acceptance of this prize means/ we are alive/ anybody cd
see us now/ we're here on earth/ human beings . . .

*michael*
awright then/ continue. & this time i wanta see you tell em straight out
that you are/ osiris returned & yr camera has been the missing organ in
our forsaken land. hail sean david/ osiris/ king of visions & dream

*sean*
uh huh. that's right gentlemen/ my photographs are the contours of life
unnoticed

*michael*
unrealized & suspect

*sean*
no buckwheat here

*michael*
no farina & topsy

*sean*
here we have the heat of our lives

*michael*
in our ordinaryness we are most bizarre

*sean*
prone to eccentricity/ even in our language

*michael*
our form is one of a bludgeoned thing/ wrapped in rhinestones & gauze/
blood almost sparkling/ a wildness lurks always

*sean*
a wildness lurks always

*michael*
blood almost sparkling . . . i feel like dancing the sun out the sky

*sean (twirls her, picks her up, starts to carry her to bedroom)*
& i'm gonna help you michael . . . i'm gonna help you

*(earl enters)*

*earl*
hey man/ what are you doing to nevada?

*sean (putting michael down)*
i aint doing nothing to nevada

*(michael moves to sean's desk/ puts sean's hat on)*

*earl*
i've never seen her like this/ even when she waz throwing the hammers n
nails at you/ she waz coherent/ so i brought her over to patch things up.
sean/ dont treat her regular. nevada is not commonplace/ she's right
downstairs & i'm going to get her . . .

*(michael exits to bedroom)*

*sean*
she's where?

94/

*earl*
she's downstairs/ she begged me to come talk some sense to you abt these
women

*sean*
look. earl. i dont want her up here. she is like death. dont/ dont bring her
around & dont listen to her/ she's got no place in my life

*earl*
what are you talking abt no place in yr life/ how do you think you've been
living/ on yr checks from esquire/ or claire's pussy?

*sean (grabs earl)*
look man/ dont ever say anything like that again

*earl*
oh sean/ you cant forget how colored you are for a minute. nevada dont
know what she's got herself into

*sean*
i know nevada is usedta graciousness/ & soft-spoken folk. oh/ yes a
marvelous afternoon/ & a brilliant bridge game/ dont you think/ shit. why
dont you go on & take it/ she's probably just crass enuf to manipulate you
some clients/ investments & contacts/ ahh hahahaha/ you know/ friends of
the family . . .

*earl*
no. that's not what i'm trying to do. i dont want to break up anything
tween you & nevada/ but you & i have been friends since

*sean*
since we cd hide neath mary susan's window in the projects & watch her
undress

*earl*
yeah. & rip off alla the other kids' money saying we wd do their
homework for em/ for a price/ or a kiss/ sometimes even a peek & a quarter

*sean*
so/ since you made the best of our situation/ & find yrself a professional
man now/ why dont you take nevada off my hands/ i dont have what she
needs

95/

*earl*

no/ man. that's not where i've gotten myself to/ takin yr women cuz yr
having a hard time

*sean*

since when?

*earl*

you've been stealing my women now/ i guess all the way from poly high
thru state college/ i waz always hooking up wit the one you just left/ i
cdnt figure if it waz the way i looked/ that i studied too much or waz just
scared. i waz never more brave than during the strike/ i held this lil ol
thing up on the wall/ & kisst her temples & whispered/ i dont know when
i'm gonna wander back from this assignment/ & i am in need of something
only a revolutionary woman cd give me . . .

*sean*

heh hehheh/ you didnt/ you didnt/ i never wd have believed it

*earl*

yes i did/ you can ask claire. & i said something bout her duty as a woman

*sean*

i sure am glad i didnt know michael then

*earl*

what is it abt michael?

*sean*

she's one beautiful woman/ beautiful woman . . . just face

*earl*

when are you gonna realize what's important? there are a million
beautiful faces/ & that cd be all there is/ too. you know/ i've been
practicing a couple of years now/ & making some money/ i waz thinking
you & i cd take a house up in the berkeley hills/ one of those glass &
redwood split levels/ witta terrace & the fog rolling in at dusk/ it cd be
like the old days sean/ when you & i were discovering & making a way for
ourselves/ we cd still do that/ cuz i can help you out now/ some. i mean
nothing to make you feel indebted/ but you cd leave those crazy bitches
alone/ claire is outta her mind/ believe me man . . .

    *sean (grabs a camera)*
hold it man/ i'm gonna do yr portrait. you got this face/ man/ i haveta
have

    *earl (sincerely flattered & hopeful)*
really man? yr gonna do a portrait of me/ like you do claire? man/ give me
the air of d'artagnan

    *sean*
have i ever failed you?

    *earl*
just take the pictures/ man

    *sean (taking pictures)*
here/ open yr shirt a lil . . . put that hat on right there/ let yr sensuality
lick the lens/ man . . . that's it. i really think you shd consider nevada/ ya
know her family cd help you a lot/ they've got all kinds of money/ from
what she says sounds like they own the state of texas

    *(earl had been posing/ begins to hear what sean is talking about & comes back to
    reality)*

that woman's gonna bring some man a whole lotta power/ & if it's not me/
might as well be you/ & we cd move from there. her daddy wd love to see
her married/ especially to a lawyer/ he might even give you one of his
insurance companies for a wedding present/ he knows nevada's gotta be
paid for/ she cant give much

    *(lights down on sean & earl)*

S C E N E  X I

    *(nevada, on sean's porch daydreaming, still taking sips from her flask)*

    *nevada*
mama mama/ is he gonna be like daddy?
is he gonna buy me pretty things & take me
round the world? mama/ will he be handsome
& strong/ maybe from memphis/ an old family
of freedmen/ one of them reconstruction senators
for a great grandfather/ maybe he'll buy me an orchid
a silver orchid for my cotillion/ do you think

i'm pretty enuf/ mama/ for a man like that?
i'm gonna haveta get a figure
aw ya know mama like you/ i wanna set my table
pour the punch & make canapes/ & smile like you
in an organza dress/ he cd swing me
down by the lake/ & then he'll catch me almost
in the air/ & rustle my dress round my shoulders
not like he knew he cd take such a liberty
just outta he cdnt resist me
& then mama/ then i think he'll kiss me
yeah/ there on the swing in the air
by the lake/ he'll kiss me mama
& whisper nevada . . . nevada

*(lights fade)*

## S C E N E   X I I

*(sean & earl are in same positions as before)*

*sean*
hmmmm. i shda taken that shot of her that morning when she waz
hysterical. shit/ i missed it

*earl*
now i told you i waznt interested/ besides we havent discussed that idea i
had abt our house/ you know the bachelors' haven

*sean*
no we havent & we wont/ cuz michael & i are gonna get a place in the
berkeley hills

*earl*
man/ you absolutely amaze me

*sean*
of course i do.

*earl*
now i told you nevada is downstairs

*michael (enters from bedroom/ speaking)*
so she shd go away

            *earl*
hey/ it's just she's losing her mind & we have to help her get back her
sanity

        *sean*
sanity? she's always been crazy/ she'll get tired & go home/ dont worry abt
her man

            *michael*
earl/ how you been doing anyway

            *(claire enters)*

            *claire*
oh my/ so yr both waiting for me/ how lovely

            *(claire crosses to bed/ notices earl)*

i've got something for you/ earl/ & you too/ michael

            *earl (crosses to exit)*
i dont want nothing you got

            *claire (following earl)*
that's always been yr problem

            *earl (seeing nevada at door)*
oh shit

            *nevada*
i waznt gonna come up here/ earl. sean/ i swear/ but that cheap bitch/ she
came up & i cdnt sit in the car anymore

            *(michael moves threateningly toward nevada)*

dont throw me out/ please sean/ dont throw me out

            *claire (getting between nevada and michael)*
he wdnt throw you out/ sweetheart. you look ill

            *michael*
sean/ we dont have to do this anymore

        *99/*

*(michael tries to exit to bedroom. sean follows hugs her after grabbing her by her arms to make her listen)*

*claire (to nevada)*
can i get you something

*nevada*
leave me alone/ you slut/ just leave me alone

*sean (to michael who is still distraught in his arms)*
it's okay/ nothings gonna happen/ it's gonna be awright

*(nevada tries to follow sean)*

*earl (grabbing nevada)*
claire cant hurt you/ nevada/ so why dont you just lighten up

*claire (to nevada)*
here/ have some jack daniels/ i'll get you one of her houserobes

*michael (to sean)*
they're crazy/ sean/ i dont wanna be crazy/ make it stop/ make it stop

*(sean rocks michael in embrace, soothing her)*

*claire (to nevada)*
you can read this/ the three musketeers by alexandre dumas

*(claire has poked book at nevada/ nevada tries to grab claire. earl intercedes)*

*sean (to michael)*
you're not crazy/ michael/ you're not crazy/

*(michael tries to pull away from him)*

listen michael/ i'm gonna take care of it/ it's gonna be awright/ you'll see

*(sean leads michael out to bedroom)*

*earl*
now nevada/ you have known abt claire all along. remember i usedta say/ sean needed a lot & some things you wdnt give

*nevada*
sure/ I wdnt walk around naked with other people in the room/ or stick
feathers up my crotch/ let him pour whiskey all over me

*earl*
but it's more than that/ nevada. claire comes whenever sean calls/ she
makes love in cars & trolleys/ you shd be grateful to her/ actually

*claire*
say thank you/ nevada/ say thank you

*earl*
she's not scared of sean's quirks/ so you dont haveta be bothered with his
seamy side

(*michael comes running from the bedroom screaming*)

*michael*
you all aren't in this/ get out/ go away/

(*sean right behind michael, trying to take her back to the bedroom*)

*sean*
i told you i'd take care of it/ now come listen to me/

*michael*
they are still here/ what more do you have to say

*sean*
i love you

*michael*
you love me

(*they leave for the bedroom whispering*)

*nevada* (*watching sean & michael, but speaking to earl*)
when he gets famous/ he wont haveta have anything to do with trash like
these simple-minded bitches

*claire* (*to area where sean & michael had been*)
uhuh/ you dont wanna do this

101/

*nevada (replying to claire unwittingly)*
what are you talking abt/ the only reason sean hasnt moved outta this rat
trap & taken his place in the world he belongs in/ is cuz he's got too much
pride

*claire*
you call taking yr money/ havin too much pride?

*earl*
claire/ shut up

*claire*
oh no/ let's have miss society experience some real low down nigger shit

*earl*
why dont you mind me/ claire

*claire*
i dont have to mind you/ i do what i want. i'm not above that

*nevada*
yr not above or below anything/ yr filth

*claire*
how come i know/ sean aint never tried to get no show or no
recommendations or nothing/ & you dont/ tell me nevada/ does he lie to
you all the time or just when he wants money?

*nevada*
yr ridiculous/ sean is a fine artist

*claire*
aint he/ though

*nevada*
i know you havent much training/ but i cant see how you cd play with
sean's work

*claire*
guess what/ nevada

*earl*
claire/ lay off

102/

*claire*
no no/ i want nevada to understand that i understand that sean's a niggah/
& that's why he's never gonna be great or whatever you call it/ cuz he's a
niggah & niggahs cant be nothing

*nevada*
see/ earl/ she's totally claimed by her station/ she cant imagine anyone
growing thru the prison of poverty to become someone like sean

*claire*
sean aint nothing but a niggah

(sean enters)

*sean*
is that so

*claire*
nevada/ i didnt know you liked niggahs

*sean*
she cant keep her hands off em

*nevada*
sean/ we can work this all out

*sean*
there's nothing to work out/ nevada

*earl*
arent you being a lil hard on yrself/ nevada/ i mean we've all been rejected
at one time or another

*claire*
you oughtta know

*sean*
so you know abt earl

(no one listens to him)

*nevada*
i just want to help you

103/

sean
nevada/you need help

earl
sean/ why dont you sit down & have a drink? nevada/ you are everything
sean wanted from the time we were just kids/ he wanted the girl from the
right family with good manners/ who knew something sides being felt up
& having babies/ he wanted somebody who had been someplace

sean
where you been/ earl

earl
you help him work out his visions

sean
earl/ why are you doing this?

claire
but he feels his visions right over here

nevada
no/ that's not true/ i can love him/ he knows i love him/ yall are just cheap
& usedta nothing/ that's what he comes from & he doesnt want to leave
what he thinks he belongs to/ for a good & decent life.

sean
he who nevada/ who you talking abt

nevada
he's bound to his past cuz yall remind him/ he was nothing once too/ not
you earl/ i know you changed yrself but that cheap bitch

claire
actually nevada i'm very expensive/ why i havent paid my rent for two
years/ much less mine & my man's

nevada
see earl/ i always told you she waz kept

earl
nevada dont say that/ yr making a mistake

*sean*
it's no mistake.

*claire*
oh no. its awright/ you see nevada/ men just give me things. i never asked
a man cept sean for anything/ they just give me things. that's why i can
afford to love sean/ cuz he cant give me nothing but what you awready
gave him/ so i guess that means/ i'm sporting you

*(claire grabs nevada & kisses her on the mouth)*

*earl*
that waznt necessary/ claire

*nevada (in shock)*
my god/ yr a lesbian

*claire*
oh yeah/ i dont think that's what sean thinks

*(sean goes to desk, watches them in disbelief)*

*nevada (searching thru purse)*
well/ what do you want?

*claire (closing purse)*
how abt a lil kiss

*nevada*
oh no/ leave me alone

*claire (grabs nevada)*
what's a matter/ dont you like the way i look?

*(michael enters/ joins sean at desk. earl grabs claire by the arm)*

look you faggot muthafuckah get yr hands off me

*(claire shoves earl)*

i dont like a man who doesnt like women

*earl*
now claire/ not wanting you/ has nothing to do with other women

105/

claire
dont "now claire" me/ look nevada i know what sean likes & he likes
watching women/ so you wanna help sean/ you wanna help me make sean
happy/ he's always told me he wd take yr picture/ if he cd get you with a
woman

nevada
no. no/ sean wdnt want me to do something indecent

claire
well/ now we all know why yr not enuf/ dont we nevada

earl
please stop this. nevada cant take this sorta thing

claire
well you cant either/ so hush up

earl
one of these days i'm gonna fuck you til you bleed

claire
are you gonna do it now/ earl

sean
you all shut up/ i cant do nothing more with a nymphomaniac & a
hysteric. earl move your faggot ass on, man. you all get out.

(no one moves but earl who jumps at sean. sean pushes him away.)

sean (to claire)
yeah you/ the one & only/ you wd kiss anybody/ huh to make believe
somebody loves you/ & nobody does/

claire (moving to fondle michael/ who is abt to stop her)
somebody will always love me

sean (grabbing claire)
earl/ get them outta here. take them wherever it is you go.

earl
man/ yr outta yr mind

106/

*claire (to sean)*
earl cant help me do a damn thing

*earl*
what am i/ yr clean up my shit slave or something? i thot i waz yr friend

*sean*
then be my friend & help me

*earl*
i dont want nothing to do with yr black ass

*sean*
cuz you cant keep a woman on yr own/ muthafuckah/ get that bitch there/
nevada is abt yr speed

*earl*
sean/ we really have nothing in common

*(earl exits. claire crosses to bed as if she planned to stay)*

*sean (to nevada)*
what are you doin here?

*claire (rushes to nevada and takes her arm)*
c'mon nevada

*nevada (to sean)*
i just wanted to talk to you alone

*(claire pulls nevada out the door)*

*michael*
i told you abt watching dead folks, sean

*sean (very much alone. not looking at michael)*
michael

*michael*
yes

*sean*
i am gonna be the greatest photographer in the world

107/

*michael*
i know

*sean*
my photographs are the contours of life unnoticed

(*michael begins to whisper the lines*)

unrealized & suspect/ no buckwheat here
no farina & topsy/ here we have the heat of our lives
in our ordinaryness we are most bizarre/ prone to
eccentricity/ even in our language . . . michael

(*michael stops whispering. sean realizes she is not "with him" & moves toward her, saying:*)

you are space & winds/ like a soft rain or a torrent
of dust/ you're gonna dance for everybody burdened
michael/ you can move/ you are space & winds

(*michael begins to dance*)

you are space & winds/ you . . . i do love you

*michael*
what?

*sean*
you heard me

*michael*
tell me again

*sean*
i love you

*michael (hugging sean)*
you know/ alexandre dumas had a thing for dancers/ too

(*lights fade*)

# boogie woogie landscapes

# C A S T

*layla*   an afro-american woman, 20–30. the visions, dreams & memories in this play are hers. she must be able to dance.

*night-life companions* (n.l.c.—dream-memories):

*n.l.c. #1*   young woman, should move well.

*n.l.c. #2*   a woman.

*n.l.c. #3*   older woman, should be able to sing.

*n.l.c. $4*   a man, *layla's* lover.

*n.l.c. #5*   young man, should sing & move well.

*n.l.c. #6*   a man, must be a dancer.

Presented as a 1-woman piece at the New York Shakespeare Festival's *Poetry at the Public* series on December 18, 1978.

Presented in play form at the Symphony Space Theatre, June 26, 1979, as a fund-raiser for The Frank Silvera Writer's Workshop with the following personnel:

Director, *Avery Brooks*. Choreographer, *Dianne McIntyre*. Costumes, *Beverly Parks*. Light Design, *Victor En Yu Tan*. Set Design, *McArthur Binion*. Sound, *Sharon Combs*. Stage Manager, *Malik*. Musical Director and Composer, *Baikida E. J. Carroll*. Cast: John Parks, Sam Jackson, Judye Brandt, Dyane Harvey, Matthew Bernard Johnson, Trazana Beverly, Elbert Watson, Laurie Carlos, Mary Alice, Jaqueline Yancey, Ntozake Shange. Musicians: *Baikida E. J. Carroll*, trumpet & flugelhorn, *Donald Smith, Anthony Davis*, piano, *Akua Dixon*, cello, *Wesley Brown*, bass.

this is a geography of whimsy, fantasy, memory & the night: a bedroom. the bedroom of layla ("born at night": arabic), an all-american colored girl. there is what furniture a bedroom might accommodate, though not too much of it. the most important thing is that a bedroom is suggested: the windows that overlook somewhere; an object that might be a bed; another that might be a night table. the mirrors that we see ourselves in/ comin in or goin out/ in our full regalia or in layers of our own sweat.

the walls of the bedroom are designed to permit at least one or two of the night-life companions (dream-memories) to enter or exit at will. they cd just as easily come from beneath the bed or behind curtains, from under a chair, etc., but that wd not be appropriate to the night-life of an adult, and layla is an adult when we begin.

aside from the night-life companions, layla also entertains a trio of musicians. the musicians sometimes reflect her consciousness, but more often than not, they side with the night-life interlopers, attempting to refine layla's perceptions of herself and her past.

*(layla enters her bedroom, to music we will recognize as her theme song. she is obviously returning from a night at the disco. this is revealed by her clothing, the movements she makes (as if she were dancing alternately with 3 or 4 different partners), & by musical quotations laced thru her theme. the band enters virtually thru the walls, giving us the first instance of the presence of spirits & an attitude toward life that makes fantasies tangible. layla dances to recreate her evening & to explore her present feelings which include a sense of dislocation & confusion, for the disco is over & she is in her bedroom with 3 made-up musicians. layla takes notice of the audience. begins)*

*layla*
dontcha wanna be music/ dontcha wanna be music/ dontcha wanna
be daybreak & ease into fog/ a cosmic event like sound/ & rain
yah/ like rain
like when a woman can walk down gold street
feeling like she's moved to atlantis
when the mine's been closed a hundred years
& the only gold is music seepin thru fog
it's what we call a marine intrusion
interlopin visions & lost deities findin the way home
cuz we dont recognize what's sacred anymore

oh dontcha wanna be music n ease on into the fog/ like
rain & sun/ like daybreak/ dontcha wanna be . . .

*(the six night-life companions (n.l.c.) enter thru the walls, chanting in unison at first)*

n.l.c.'s *(in unison)*
she is trapped in black & white/ she is trapped in black & white

layla *(to n.l.c.'s; she is startled & defensive)*
dontcha wanna be music & ease into the fog?
dontcha wanna be like rain/ like a cosmic event . . .

n.l.c. #2
she never thought people places or ideas were anything
but black & white

*(layla is overwhelmed by the visitors/ who take charge & begin to act out their stories)*

n.l.c. #1
a macadam road & black bark trees
singed grass in soot dirt & a house
more like a cave/ she's black too
not tar like but a shade lighter than
the sky that envelops her legs while
she walks/ headlights frighten her
where she is from the sun is ochre
& daylight no different from sleep/
her most serious problem is how
to stop walking on this road the
color of pitch/ this path slippin off
exploration with long sticks leads nowhere/
she is trapped in black & white/ without shadows
she cannot lean against anything/
the earth has no depth because she cannot hold it
she cannot go away/ the horizon implies three dimensions

n.l.c. #3
if she were to try to bump into a tree/ she
wd go thru it unmarked/ no things
have taste/ or weight/ she is as facile
as air at 14 years old/ she wonders if
anyone has penetrated the chiaroscuro of her life
she is a deeper gray than the shutters of her house.

n.l.c. #2
her hair tangles the wind like billie holiday's voice/
her tears fall behind her blacker than her songs/

she follows these back to her house
where she howls/ for anything red.

    *layla*
inside the cave i imagine i can
cook something to eat/ but my hands dont work
the skillet burns up/ my mother's smoke
scars my arms/ my mouth blurts some phrase
i wd have a fierce yellow
but i dont know what that is.

    *n.l.c. #4*
she tries to stumble on something to stop
this charcoal life/ she goes from room to room
like a tractor in the grapes of wrath/ but
everything she touches gets blacker & more nondescript/
"that's it"/ she says

    *layla*
smudges/ i'm soft graphite
i'm clumsy & reckless/ i'm a hazard to definitions

    *n.l.c. #5*
she threw herself on her bed & her sobs
roused her so/ she began to beat the walls
her fists matted the surface with grime/
she turned to the doors/ rubbin her face
across the thresholds/ she created ebony blurs
that she cdnt even reach less she leave a furrow
of slate fingerprints/ she made things black

    *n.l.c. #6*
indistinguishable. only someone else accustomed to
overwhelming darkness/ cd see her under the bed
tryin not to wipe her tears
she didnt want anything as black as the palms of her hands
to touch her

    *n.l.c. #1*
she waz black enuf awready/ dawns held no surprises.

    *layla*
i feel like an oven

n.l.c. #1

all black & crusty/ with a huge space to fill up
with something/ she ate newspapers/ the black & white pages/
thinking news of the outside world wd soothe her hunger.
but she started to eat her books/ even the gothic novels/
the frank yerby slaves/ made her ill/ but she chewed
*foxes of harrow* & swallowed *mandingo*/ like her joy
she had hidden these pages in a great box under her bed/
no one understood where the newspapers disappeared to/
but she knew it didnt matter/ cuz the outside world waz
black & white & thin like where she lived. she cd
read in the dark/ & eventually only ate *the new york times*/
the newsprint of the *times* waznt cheap like local papers
or gritty like the *philadelphia inquirer*
but as she tore the pages/ HELP WANTED first/ then
REAL ESTATE/ stuffing them in her mouth/ she never thought
people places or ideas were anything but black & white/
no one printed books in colors/ plus she waznt sure
what colors were/ till she discovered jesus/ on the radio/
the voice/ with cadence like her grandma's
but deep / & husky.

n.l.c. #4

hello jesus/ jesus is with us tonite
& there is a great light shining in yr soul.

*layla*
amen/ amen.

n.l.c. #2

as jesus came closer to her heart the way
the deep voice waz sayin/ she knew the sun waz yellow
& warm/ cuz the sun got in her throat & pushed a brilliant
glow of shout from her/ not only heaven/ but the world
waz bathed in the gold of his love. she ran in the
sunlight of herself thru the house praisin god/
lettin her laughter wash thru the darkness of night.

n.l.c. #6

& she stood in a arc of yellow so bright
her mother came runnin to see what waz the matter/
even tho the child had laid a daffodil glaze
to the whole house/ the mother cd not see

116/

jesus had released her to the warmth of herself.
the mother waz cold/ & thought the rush of color
from her daughter's mouth/ too blazing & niggardly
for her household. no more deep voices on the radio.

### n.l.c. #3
no/ jesus does not like noise/ & his light shines
in the church & the blessing & the lord's prayer
using trespasses/ not debts. we owe no debts.

### n.l.c. #2
& the daffodils crawled back into the child's mouth
but she never forgot again that even if jesus
didnt hear her sayin hello/ something made her wanna
say hello/ cuz she had a glowin inside her that changed the world.
now she cd touch her face with the palms of her hands
she usedta sit on/ those black hands
now caressed her with forsythia delicacy
her soul waz filled with daffodils/ tulips spread in her cheeks.

### layla
i waz growin beyond this singed & reluctant plane/
i discovered dimensions/ & hope.

### n.l.c. #4
there are horizons. there are different dawns.

### n.l.c. #3
not here/ but out there somewhere/ or maybe
in my hands/ these black hands.

### n.l.c. #5
the corn waz yellow/ under the heavy sheaths of husk
the corn waz yellow/ as she was bright under the crust
of herself. the sunrise was piqued with gold
like her voice winding thru the limbs of trees
on the thin road she no longer walked/ she sailed
the gravel & the sticks she held as a mast for herself.
at the door/ she drew in all this color.
the spinach was ashen still & the grim boilin water
for black teas/ greeted her with cackles, shrieks &
ignorance of her tastes/ once under the bed & starving
she let out a gust of light/ & lay it about her like

other girls she didnt know might have lined up their dolls/
she studied the legs & arms of herself/ the hair & lips
of herself/ before the burst of spirit let her hold herself.

n.l.c. #3
she had withdrawn from the hugs of her mother her father
her grandmother & those other lil blk things who lived with her/
the sisters & brothers who had found no colors/
who still left huge slurs of gray all around/
she held herself in her light/ feeling sorry for the rest.
if she let them near her/ they might smudge this precious secret/
this soft fire she waz/ she wd never do that/ she waz selfish
she wd never even tell them there waz something more
than black & white skinny lives & black & white shutters/
& black cries & white yelps/ she wd never tell them
but/ as she thought these black & white thoughts/
she heard the lil blk things/ brothers & sisters/
making sounds like horses surrounded by coyotes/
sounds like Rodan & someone falling from a 16th floor
thru the glass/ to sidewalks/ sounds like a crowd/
peering at smashed bodies.

n.l.c. #1
she ran/ she ran leaving blurts of yellow & smudges of gray
thru the halls. everything she touched as she stumbled
toward the noise waz golden & black/ she had forgotten to
put her spirit back/ she ran into a wave of heat
she had never felt/ a rush of scarlet came cross her body/
threw her over the porch to reach the ankle of one of
the little black things. red/ she saw red/ & the lil
black things' tears were orange as she grabbed their faces
& her brightness wiped the fire from their brows/
they were charred now/
as thin scrawny cheap white men made down the road
laughin out the windows of their thin scrawny truck.

n.l.c.'s (in unison)
niggahs/ niggahs/ go home/ go home/ niggahs!

n.l.c. #6
the lil black things/ pulled to her & whimpered lil black whys/
"Why did those white men make red of our house/ why did those
white men want to blacken even the white doors of our house/

why make fire of our trees/ & our legs/ why make fire/
why laugh at us/ say go home/ arent we home/ arent we home?''

n.l.c. #2
she saw red. she saw senseless blazes in her arms.
carrying the lil black things into the house/ the black
& white house/ the smudges of children were a cacophony
of colors. now they all knew/ if you can see black
you can see/ yellow/ that softness/ that glow that wipes tears
& holds close/ but holding soft & close/ means danger/
makes you see red/ to orange/ to make fury
to champion the tendermost.

layla
i drew the lil black things with me under my bed
& wiped the scarlet stains from their mouths
with the light of myself.

n.l.c. #4
even these smudges of children/ these lil black things/
cdnt dim the brightness of her. she cd tell them/
but even she didnt know why
the thin scrawny white men in a truck laughin
had made a fire/ to char these black limbs
til they fell abt the fields/ like dry old leaves.

n.l.c. #2
she got too big to hide under her bed/
she didnt really want to hide any more.
the warmth of her waz sought & cherished by the smudges
of children/ even they shared the lil color they had dug
from themselves/ the glow & the ravage of red/
the orange leaps that spattered cross the sky.
there waz the thin black road & the frail charcoal of dusk here/
but morning breeze curved their lips & left the treasured
azure hue of dreams on their cheeks. she grew to expect colors/
& the memories of acres of indistinguishable black mosses/
walls of shadow creepin between/ long thin steps/
her own dark paths/ & the hungers she knew that opaque night
the thin white men in a truck/ spread sick crimson round her mouth/
the blue of dream in her arms/ these violet memories
rounded her body so/ gave depth to her gaze.
she waz too full for black & white & skinny life
besides/ her eyes were chestnut brown.

119/

    *n.l.c.'s (in unison)*
she waz too full for a black & white & skinny life
she waz too full for a black & white & skinny life

    *layla (underneath them)*
when a woman can walk down gold street
feelin like she's moved to atlantis
when the mine's been closed a hundred years
& the only gold is music seepin thru fog
it's what we call a marine intrusion.
interlopin visions & lost deities/ findin the way home/
like thieves/ cuz we dont recognize what's sacred anymore

    *n.l.c.'s (in unison, under layla, as they exit)*
remember what's sacred/ what's sacred anymore/ remember
what's sacred/ anymore?

    *layla (cont'd)*
women in big hats wit lilies behind their ears
women in blk & white scarves dance on stairways with
bougainvillea & clouds/ men in jeans & honest faces.
music offers solace/ offers some kinda way to reach out/
to ring bells on gold street/ not tin pan alley
but montezuma's preciousness/ a marine intrusion
natural as tides/ learnin to pray. to give more of yrself
than ya think ya have/ diggin below the bottom of what's possible/
& so clean/ like a expensive gangster/ a tibetan shaman's
prophesy/ marine intrusion/ like wind
like winds make fires/ make dust swirl
make us catch ourselves/ fly against our will
til we like it/ til we know we waz meant to soar/
to be free/ in truth/ in silence.
more ourselves & music/ like a voice we cannot speak in/
a voice to move thru/ more than heart
marine intrusion's a meteorological phenomenon/ like rain
like rain & sun/ like c'mon       c'mon

the consequence of bein real/ unpredictable as the weather
sure as the sun risin/ the sweet comeuppance of risk . . .
if ya wear a lotus in yr hair/ it'll fly wit the horn
to another space. marine intrusion movin soft movin strong/
you cant hurt ya.
dontcha wanna be music/ dontcha wanna be/ dontcha wanna/
dontcha wanna be daybreak & ease into fog/ a cosmic event/
sound/ & rain. yeah/ like rain.

> (layla is relieved that the excitement has ceased. she is alone again, having
> convinced us that we can join in her reveries. she becomes languid, and prepares for
> bed, i.e., sleep. enter n.l.c. #4, the man who loves her)

### n.l.c. #4
you drink continually from a scarlet wine glass
& let yr brazziere straps slip/ round/ yr shoulders
yr hair is acorns/ yr hair is like a bundle of dreads
round up on themselves/ you sit on glass & look at us
with eyes as unfamiliar as your simplicity.
you rest your hands on light/ make yrself/ over & over
you are your own mirror/ yr own déjà-vu/ i, yr accomplice.
yr beauty is irreducible/ yr hair acorns.

### layla (nonchalantly)
as a child i threw these brown concentric miracles
to the bears in the park where colored children cd play/
as a child i knew acorns as toys/ as the ends of trees
i cd not climb.

### n.l.c. #4
yr hair is acorns/ you rest on glass/ quick
as a sailboat heeling/ yr wine glass barely braizes yr lips/
vermelho tambem/ yr nails unpainted/ ridiculously inviting
you sit here in carved glass/ in mirrors/ on light/
in sepia caves/ only i imagine/ i sleep near you
you are not afraid of the dark/ the wine simply eases
the flowers from yr cheeks to my dreams/ the red goblet
signals my white stallions to trot
now/ we are ready for the vision/ we are the silk blossoms
of the fica/ needin sun/ lil water/ daily care.

### layla
my feet get dirty sometimes/ i like to walk in soil.

121/

n.l.c. #4
you sit on embroidered glass in a beige brazziere/
you can do without seashells.

layla
i am sometimes naked/ but mostly i wear my past/
the pinafores & white socks that shamed me.

n.l.c. #4
this woman with acorn hair/ can be caressed
can stimulate even men with leica eyes
you drink "du vin blanc bon" on glass so old
even white men approach with reverence.
my lover/ the acorn hair woman.

layla
how i've known myself among you.

n.l.c. #4
the one whose head cd not be touched/ the woman too tough
to tossle & fling to the sky/ who rests on glass
& mirrors/ light/ memory/ the woman with no red lights.

layla
only a red glass/ full of love.

n.l.c. #4
a red glass so close to yr lips/ not unlike a kiss
not at all like my lips/ but constant & always possible.
you put yr hope where you can have it
you sleep with me on laced glass/ in caves swollen with beauty/
i put my dreams in yr goblet.

layla
i sleep more easily now/ my love in that scarlet cup.

(n.l.c. #4 exits)
i can almost taste you/ my brazziere/ fallin from my shoulder.
i almost believe/ you gave me this.

(layla looks hoping to see the man who loves her, but instead there are two women,
very agitated & aggressive, coming toward her. layla tries to gather her clothes,
crouches near what might be her bed)

### n.l.c. #1
what are they gonna do/ take the windows & doors from
our houses/ leave us lil boxes no man can enter for fear of
electrocution/ bar us from the streets/ at threat of
life imprisonment: alternative number 1: all the men
are locked in boxes with no windows & no doors/ we can come
& go as we please/ at any hour/ any day.

### n.l.c. #3
alternative number 2: all the men are sent to new jersey
& the women's army air corps guards all tunnels & bridges/
airport, bus & train stations to make sure that no men invade
the state during rape prevention month. since there are
actually 50 states in the union/ i imagine we cd pair off
& alternate during the year/ so at any time maybe some 25
states wd be free of rape for a month.

### n.l.c. #1
all the yng men who go to cuba & come back with stories about
how the yng women in cuba walk abt with no fear in their streets/
these yng men are sent out in the streets of new york
with bull horns. they are given prime time 60-second spots
to tell eyewitness news the story of how there is no rape
in cuba. the city of new york supplies transportation for
the thousands of women in the boxes/ or for the thousands
of women waiting for the men to go to new jersey/ to go to
cuba where rape is treason.

### n.l.c. #3
women shd go everywhere in 2's after dark. women who dont
have friends or want to take a walk alone/ have to stay in
or getta police dog. also women walking alone/ or rather
in 2's after dark/ must counter rumors that the only thing
2 women wd want to do without a man is to fuck each other/
in this case/ they are still preventing rape.

### n.l.c. #1
self-defense classes are offered free by the state during
working hours to all women. self-defense classes are given
in the streets to all unemployed women. self-defense classes
are mandatory for our children/ from age 3/ to prevent rape.

### n.l.c. #3
every convicted rapist must be in a parade thru times square

during rape prevention month. all the porno houses will be
closed down during this parade/ no one shall be able to see
any sexual violence/ there will be the annual rapists' parade
instead.

n.l.c. #1
give us guns.

n.l.c. #3
unless the streets are made safe for us/ we shall call a
general strike/ in factories/ at home/ at school.
we shall say we cannot come to work/ it is not safe.

n.l.c. #1
rape victims are given prime time 60-second spots to say
what happened to them. the governor/ the mayor/ & the entire
city council will personally see the rape victim/ apologize
for the municipal negligence/ the failure of the state
to provide secure living space/ & the state pays for all debts
incurred by the crime they survived. in addition/ all women
who died or who demonstrated remarkable courage & integrity
during rape attacks are given congressional medals of honor.

n.l.c. #3
or the purple heart.

n.l.c. #1 & 3 (in unison)
we shall have streets/ schools & monuments named after all
these women & children/ they died for their country.

(n.l.c. #5 shouts as if he were a newsboy in the thirties)

n.l.c. #5
EXTRA EXTRA/ READ ALL ABOUT IT!
EXTRA EXTRA/ REAL ALL ABOUT IT!

(cont'd, confidentially to the audience)

the ny times has never asked me what i think abt a goddamn thing.
the ny times has never excused himself to take a leak
no/ the times has never helped in times of need
or offered his seat to a pregnant woman on the irt
as a matter of fact

at breakfast the *times* is quite rude
interruptin conversations in any language
unless i insist on sittin under the table
so i cd talk to people's knees
i've never been able to communicate with someone
whose nose is in the *times*/ also i'd like
to mention i've never seen the *times* dance
can the *ny times* dance
can the *times* get down
i mean/ in habana/ everybody knows fidel can mambo
a revolutionary rhumba/ if fidel can do it/ it
cant be so hard to love yr people n keep in step/
at the same time/ everybody in the ford assembly line
cd do it/ the folks in soweto cd do it/ i mean think
n dance at the same time/ but i've never heard tell
of the ny *times* takin notice of that moment when
"CASTRO LEADS HABANA IN NATIONAL RHUMBA" just
like they make no mention of the fact that jimmy carter
cant dance to any rhythm known to man.
(perhaps/ he cd do it on the moon/ that's aristocratic/
dont ya think/ not many people cd get there/ the secret
service wdnt have much to do/ on the moon/ all white
n barren n free of anybody who looks like me/ on the
moon jimmy carter cd do a foxtrot or some peckerwood
derivation thereof/ the ayatollah is very formal/ but
brezhnev n carter cd have the first disco contest on
the moon/ with afghanistan as the prize)
still i wd like to get the ny *times* out of my social life
the next time someone asks me if i have seen the paper/
i'll say/ i've seen more news than is fit to print
& yes we have deliveries everyday/ discounts to
households that understand the rhythm of our lives
n speak colloquial universal language/ we go
person to person/ block to block/ any way ya wanna get it
any way ya wanna get it/ we got it
EXTRA EXTRA READ ALL ABOUT IT:
ZIMBABWE CELEBRATES FIFTY YEARS OF INDEPENDENCE
EXTRA EXTRA READ ALL ABOUT IT:
THOUSANDS OF WRITERS FLOCK TO INTERNATIONAL CONFERENCE
ON FREE SPEECH IN ARGENTINA
EXTRA EXTRA READ ALL ABOUT IT:
WHITE SOUTH AFRICANS DENIED ENTRY TO THE UNITED STATES
AS WAR CRIMINALS

EXTRA EXTRA READ ALL ABOUT IT:
NOT ONE AFRO-AMERICAN CHILD WHO CANT READ & WRITE/
CELEBRATION OF CAMPAIGN AGAINST NATIONAL ILLITERACY
EPIDEMIC HELD IN BED-STUY
that's how i see it, today. now that's the news that's
fit to print.
EXTRA EXTRA READ ALL ABOUT IT/
EXTRA EXTRA READ ALL ABOUT IT

*(then fanfare hits like at the apollo for the james brown review. n.l.c. #5, who is an
r&b star, enters—or rather, leaps in)*

   n.l.c. #6
can i have a word        the word wid you        like the spinners
waz talkin bout a MIGHTY LOVE
MIGHTY MIGHTY MIGHTY MIGHTY LOVE

   *layla*
that grabs me/ i'm thinkin black & realizin colored.
cant stand no man to be callin me BABEE to my face

   n.l.c. #1
but if i hear some stylistics du-wah
BETCHA BY GOLLY WOW to me/ dontcha know i wanna give it away!
baby: YOU MAKE ME FEEL SO BRAND NEW . . . so brand new.

   n.l.c. #3
& there's another strut i cant do widout:
satiné suits & lamé cuffs/ volcano blue crepe shirts
& heavy chests/ like muhammad ali gone & learned
to charm a lady/ sweep a child to womanhood/ from the stage
make mama scream/ & she dont know that man's name.

   n.l.c.'s & layla *(in unison, singing from WHY DO FOOLS FALL IN
   LOVE)*
UE WAH UE WAH EU WAH OW HAAAAaaa

   n.l.c. #1
the audacity of the blues! rock me daddy/ roll me daddy
rock n roll me at the bijou/ de uptown/ in soldan's gym
saw jackie tear his shirt/ throw it to us/
smokey leanin over de lights/ sighin for us

126/

*n.l.c. #5*
oo OO ooooooo baby babeeeee. . . . .

*n.l.c.'s & layla (in unison, singing)*
LET ME BUILD YOU A CASTLE . . .

*layla*
bring all the hornplayers i know/ gonna sing & shout
like the babysitter's tryin to entertain us/

*n.l.c. #3*
do the chicken. do the slop. chantels gonna chiffon
& pearl appliqué theyselves all over dis room

*n.l.c. #1 (singing)*
& MAYBE      IF I PRAY EVERY DAY      YOU'LL COME BACK TO
ME

*n.l.c.'s & layla (in unison)*
& i'ma rock      & i'ma roll

*n.l.c. #3*
in all of them free music blues.

*n.l.c. #5*
joseph bowie knows what i'm talkin bout/
the art ensemble jumped the r&b train headin for saturn
on saturday nite is colored/ i aint lyin

*n.l.c. #1*
& them flyin capes/ exaggerated broken hearts/ teasin me
when the drifters go down them railroad tracks
there she goes

*n.l.c.'s & layla (in unison, singing)*
THERE GOES MY BABY      MOVIN ON DOWN THE LINE

*n.l.c. #5*
archie & frank lowe/ whatchu blowin bout?
there she goes      there she goes.

*n.l.c. #3 (singing)*
IT'S A BLK & BLUE HOLIDAY

*n.l.c. #5*
in atlantic city/ club harlem/ bein colored on the 4th of july!

*n.l.c.'s & layla (in unison, singing)*
& I'MA LOOKIN     I'M LOOKIN     I'M LOOKIN
OH LOOKIN FOR A LOVE     TO CALL MY OWN

*n.l.c. #3*
& i aint particular/ what kinda guitar you got
long as/ you can play me/ that song

*layla*
rock me     daddy     roll me     daddy
bring me them rhythms & blues
i'ma neo-afrikan lady BUT:

*n.l.c.'s & layla (à la O. Redding SATISFACTION)*
I GOTTA GOTTA GOTTAGOTTA

*n.l.c. #5*
get me some rock & rollssss!
c'mon albert/ where are you at

*n.l.c. #3*
yeah, albert/ where are you at/ i'ma ride yr ribald squeal
like chuck berry roosters in st. louis

*n.l.c. #5*
sun-ra & horace/ bring all them heliotropical folks
to this heah ROCK N ROLL PREVIEW

*layla*
bring me some ol roots/ irresistible!

*n.l.c.'s & layla (COME GO WITH ME)*
BA DA DADA DADA DA DAD A DUMM

*n.l.c. #5*
listen, cecil mcbee

*n.l.c. #1*
listen heah/ ike turner got me all gainst the wall
& i waznt goin nowhere

*layla*
i waznt goin nowhere/ nowhere but home

*n.l.c.'s*
i waznt goin nowhere . . . nowhere but home . . . i waznt
goin nowhere . . .

*layla*
YOU BETTAH TELL SOMEBODY TO MEET ME!

*n.l.c. #3*
TELL SOMEBODY TO MEET ME & tell me somethin good . . .
tell me that you love me      YEAH
bring a lil delfonics in yr smile

*n.l.c. #1*
march clifford thornton all round in thru heah!

*n.l.c. #3*
rock me daddy

*layla*
roll me daddy

*n.l.c. #5*
deliver yrself!

*n.l.c.'s & layla (in unison, singing)*
SO FIIIINE YEEAH      MY BABY'S SO DOGGONE FINE

*n.l.c. #3*
& free/ & sing it to me/ SING it to me

*layla*
i'ma neo-afrikan lady/ but

*n.l.c.'s & layla (singing)*
I GOTTA GOTTA GOTTA GOT GOT GOTTA

*layla*
i gotta have me some of that rock n roll for de new land.

(the company freezes. enter n.l.c. #2)

129/

### n.l.c. #2

we waz a house fulla chirren who waz fulla the dickens cordin to grandma. there waz me & my 2 sisters & my brother & my 2 cousins/ too smart for our own good & nothin but trouble for the ladies who looked after us while mama waz at work & papa went to the hospital.

*(n.l.c.'s begin to mime actions as described)*

we cd watch little rock & eisenhower or american bandstand/ then wait til waz the day for colored at the Y/ or play beat-em-up in the yard. or wrestle wid the white boys from texas down the street. i usedta like to dig holes in damp ground & line the worms up on the sidewalk/ my brother liked to set things on fire/ & my sister liked to beat me up til i told on her/ then pull my top braid that wasnt pressed cuz it waz summer & a waste of money/ til some of my hair wd actually come out in her hand. my littlest sister liked to write "pussy" in nail polish behind the refrigerator/ & my cousins rode bikes

*(n.l.c.'s freeze)*

up on the private catholic girls' school til the police came/ they waz only twelve/ but the officer saw my mama waznt no regular colored woman/ so he just warned her bout the attitude folks in st. louis had toward nigras/ & since she waz from the north & her chirren waznt "customed to tradition"/ he'd let it go on by. this time.

*(n.l.c.'s begin miming action)*

well. we ran bernice off cuz she cdnt cook nothin but hard stiff grits & didnt 'low none of us to run up & down the stairs or rub the goldfish together. & she always tol mama when one of them fresh boys wd come by to talk to me on the front porch. but she never cd figure out which one of us waz stealin her change & buyin snickers & new jack sets

### n.l.c. #3

now/ which one of you is stealin my change/ & buyin snickers & new jack sets?

### n.l.c. #2

MAMA! BERNICE IS IMAGININ THINGS! so mama fired her.

*(n.l.c.'s improv gleeful goodbyes to n.l.c. #3; she exits. n.l.c.'s move stage left & sit back to back, as if under a tree)*

*n.l.c. #2*
there waz a tree in fronta the house

*(she joins the group & sits)*

alla us usedta sit by it & think of things to do. watch the earth roll under
the clouds/ waz the only time we knew peace/ cuz in the house waz
grandma

*(n.l.c. #1 gets up, moves center. she is grandma)*

raisin cain her own self/ cuz somebody rode down the street on the bike/
free-handed/ or somebody trampled mr. noble's carnations & it waz one of
us/ so there waznt no calm in the house/ til regina came.

*(layla gets up, begins dance. she is regina)*

doin the slop. listenin to tina turner. eavesdroppin on roscoe & regina
when they slipped to the side porch & waz feelin on each other. regina
waz a high-school drop-out/ but she waz pretty/ wid spit curls & big bangs
over her eyes. & she wore tight skirts & bernard's ring on a chain round
her neck. she took us to sumner high

*(n.l.c.'s rise, begin dancing)*

where the baddest basketball team for colored waz/ to see smokey
robinson & the miracles sing "shop around"/ & she let us dance on the
stage. when regina waz wid us/ even grandma let us alone. she waz so
busy seein to it that roscoe didnt stay long & regina didnt forget she waz a
lady/ grandma forgot all about us.

*(n.l.c.'s mime learning to french kiss)*

then/ in the middle of little willie john & regina's friends showin us how
to "french kiss"/ grandma came lookin for her fan. & mama fired regina for
bein a bad influence.

*(n.l.c.'s improv sad goodbyes to layla; she exits. the mime of actions continues)*

the house got crazy. mama tryin to feed nine people & make lunches for
five/ put each one of us at a different bus stop. cuz a integration/ none of
us went to the neighborhood school/ my own school was 15 miles away/
so grandma tried to help/ & she got real nervous tryin to please mama/ &

be in her room cryin cuz none of us wd mind. waz all the time sassin her. forcin her to cut switches off the hedges to whip our legs/ when we waz the only granchirren she had. i had had just about enuf & ran off a couple of times. & mr. robinson at the pharmacy by the trolley stop always called mama to tell her what line i got on/ & then the trolley driver wd stop & let a police on/ who took me back/ & i came home from mrs. maureen's fulla beauty parlor gossip a child had no right to hear/ & when i tried to listen to blues on the radio/ somebody wd turn it off

(n.l.c. #5 mimes turning radio off; he is daddy)

& 'cuse me of tryin my best to be a niggah. so mama went away

(n.l.c. #3 exits)

for a while & daddy brushed our braids to a point like a dunce's cap & then patted them down. he gave us way too much money for lunch & tol grandma she waz overworkin her heart so he wd have to get someone to come in til mama figured out whether she waz comin back.

(n.l.c.'s exit, except for #2)

it waz sposed to be a secret bout mama not bein sure whether she wanted to live wid us/ but i knew. & cuz i didnt want the others to worry & cuz they were becomin bothersome/ i didnt say nothin bout it. & when carrie came i figured everythin wd always be awright. now carrie waz a big woman/ bigger than any woman on my mama's side or daddy's/ even aunt marie who waz sposed to have talked in tongues & run a farm all by herself cdnt have been as big as carrie. & carrie straightened her hair so funny/ it made her look even bigger/ cuz she didnt curl it/ just ran a hot comb thru it/ so it pointed out in all directions/ like a white man's crew cut. & she had pierced ears/ like aunt mamie's who waz 90/ & the ears liked ta touch her shoulders/ they waz so long & narrow/ but more n alla that/ carrie wore two house dresses at the same time. one up til lunch & the other up til she went to her rooms on the top floor/ where the white folks who lived there before us/ left all this junk/ scrapbooks & crinolines & things. carrie tied her dresses wid a rope/ a real thick rope. not like one for hanging clothes/ but like one for makin a swing on a tree/ & she always wore it/ even when she changed house dresses. & carrie wdnt use none of the bathrooms/ even tho there oughtta have been enuf for her/ cuz there waz one on each floor/ but carrie usedta say/ she liked the latrine in the cellar cuz that's what her mama had in arkansas/ & that's where she went. of course, my mama didnt know that.

(n.l.c. #3 enters)

mama came home. we had a party. carrie started bein more proper/ not
cursin or drinkin so much/ & never mentionin men anymore/ it just waznt
the same/ but the house sure did run good. me & my sisters stopped
fightin in the bed/ & i didnt run off/ the boys stopped stealin things/ & my
brother started makin up songs like chuck berry steada burnin up every
thing. we usedta play like we waz the shirelles & mama wd sing christian
gospel songs

(n.l.c. #3 begins singing HIS EYE IS ON THE SPARROW)

like paul robeson/ not like the man at the church carrie took us to
sometimes/ where we cd play tambourines & get a spirit. just bout the
time vanita/ my very best friend/ got to wear stockings insteada anklets/
mama took us aside for a talk bout things women shd know/ & i checked
everything she told me wid carrie. & carrie said mama waz almost right/
but it waznt necessary to keep yr dress down/ yr knees locked/ & yr head
high/ all the time. just when some no good niggah came round did ya
need to do alla that pre-cautionin. on fridays/ carrie stayed gone til
monday mornin/ she came back just in time to help me get everybody's
lunch together & make daddy's breakfast/ cuz mama

(n.l.c. #3 exits)

skipped that meal for her figure. & i waz gettin to be real important/ cuz
carrie had shown me how to fix just about every thing we ate/ how to
starch clothes/ & wax the crevices on the stairway/ how to clean crystal &
silver/ what to say when some one called. i always usedta shout "mama,
it's somebody colored," or, "daddy it's a white man"/ but carrie showed
me how to be right/ & to sweep all under the bed & turn the blinds at
midday so the sun wdnt bleach the furniture.

(n.l.c.'s enter, begin miming the action)

so when carrie didnt come this one monday mornin, i figured i wd cover
for her. i cda done a good job, too/ cept mama & grandma kept askin
where waz carrie/ & wdnt let me do none of the stuff i knew how to do/
widout tellin me their way/ which waznt the way carrie showed me. so i
got in a fight wid em/ & they cused me of bein a impudence & not havin
respect. & as i waz movin the glasses outta the dishwasher/ to pour juice
for us/ my dumb brother dropped his shoe he cdnt tie in between my legs/
& all the glasses shattered cross the floor

        *n.l.c. #1 (holds her heart)*
lord lord. please be careful.

        *n.l.c. #3 (angry, ad lib cursing)*
goddamn! watch what yr doin . . . look what you've done . . .

        *n.l.c. #2*
& mama waz cursin/ & the phone rang.

        *(all n.l.c.'s except #2 & #3 freeze)*

        *n.l.c. #3*
carrie/ where are you?

        *n.l.c. #2*
i waz sweepin up the glass/ & carrie musta been goin round the bush/ cuz
finally mama looked sick & said

        *n.l.c. #3*
JAIL! well/ why?

        *n.l.c. #2*
i know for sure carrie said "cuz i hadta cut a friend of mine" . . .

        *n.l.c. #3*
cut a friend of yrs? cut a friend of yrs! carrie. come pick up yr things & yr
last check/ cuz there's no way in the world you cd expect me to let a
criminal look after my chirren!

        *(n.l.c.'s exit except #3, who stands frozen)*

carrie musta come while we were at school/ when i came home alla her
things were gone/ but i found some of the rope she usedta tie round her
waist by the latrine downstairs in the cellar. my sisters & my brother & my
cousins/ didnt even realize what had happened/ our losin carrie & all . . .
& i never mentioned my feelins to mama/ cuz then she wd just remind
me/ that i always pick the most niggerish people in the world to make my
friends. & then she wd list mavis & freddie & charlenetta & linda susan
(who waz really po white trash) so i didnt say nothin. i just took carrie's
place in the house/ & did everythin like she wda/ cept i did use the
regular bathrooms/ & prayed for her like she prayed for the one of her
chirren waz most dead. cdnt see how anybody didnt know carrie wdnt cut

nobody/ less they hurt her a whole lot. not less she hurt a whole lot. carrie
wdnt cut nobody/ not less they hurt her a whole lot . . . i cdnt see . . .

(n.l.c. #2 exits, repeating last lines a little)
(n.l.c. #3 turns to exit; turns back, crosses downstage)

n.l.c. #3
it's not so good to be born a girl/ sometimes.

*(she turns to exit again, & turns back)*

that's why societies usedta throw us away/ or sell us/ or play with our
vaginas/ cuz that's all girls were good for. at least women cd carry things
& cook/ but to be born a girl is not good sometimes/ some places/ such
abominable things cd happen to us. i wish it waz gd to be born a girl
everywhere/ then i wd know for sure that no one wd be infibulated/ that's
a word no one wants us to know. infibulation is sewing our vaginas up
with cat-gut or weeds or nylon thread to insure our virginity. virginity
insurance equals infibulation. that can also make it impossible for us to
live thru labor/ make it impossible for the baby to live thru labor.
infibulation lets us get infections that we cant mention/ cuz disease in the
ovaries is a sign that we're dirty anyway/ so wash yrself/ cuz once
infibulated we have to be cut open to have/ you know what/ the joy of the
phallus/ that we may know nothing about/ ever/ especially if something
else not good that happens to little girls happens: if we've been excised.
had our labia removed with glass or scissors. if we've lost our clitoris
because our pleasure is profane & the presence of our naturally evolved
clitoris wd disrupt the very unnatural dynamic of polygamy. so with no
clitoris/ no labia & infibulation/ we're sewn-up/ cut-up/ pared down & sore
if not dead/ & oozing pus/ if not terrified that so much of our body waz
wrong & did not belong on earth. such thoughts lead to a silence/ that
hangs behind veils & straightjackets/ it really is not so good to be born a
girl when we have to be infibulated, excised, clitorectomized & STILL be
afraid to walk the streets or stay home at night. i'm so saddened that being
born a girl makes it dangerous to attend midnight mass unescorted. some
places if we're born girls & someone else who's very sick & weak & cruel/
attacks us & breaks our hymen/ we have to be killed/ sent away from our
families/ forbidden to touch our children. these strange people who
wound little girls are known as attackers/ molesters & rapists. they are
known all over the world & are proliferating at a rapid rate. to be born a
girl who will always have to worry not only abt the molesters/ the
attackers & the rapists/ but also abt their peculiarities: does he stab too/ or
shoot? does he carry an axe? does he spit on you? does he know if he

doesnt drop sperm we cant prove we've been violated? these subtleties
make being a girl too complex/ for some of us & we go crazy/ or never go
anyplace. some of us have never had an open window or a walk alone,
but sometimes our homes are not safe for us either. rapists & attackers &
molesters are not strangers to everyone/ they are related to somebody/ &
some of them like raping & molesting their family members better than a
girl-child they don't know yet. this is called incest, & girl children are
discouraged from revealing attacks from uncle or daddy/ cuz what wd
mommy do? after all/ daddy may have seen to it that abortions were
outlawed in his state/ so that mommy might have too many children to
care abt some "fun" daddy might be having with the 2-yr-old/ she's a girl
after all/ we have to get used to it. but infibulation, excision,
clitorectomies, rape & incest are irrevocable life-deniers/ life stranglers &
disrespectful of natural elements. i wish these things wdnt happen
anywhere anymore/ then i cd say it waz gd to be born a girl everywhere.
even though gender is not destiny/ right now being born a girl is to be
born threatened; i want being born a girl to be a cause for celebration/
cause for protection & nourishment of our birthright/ to live freely with
passion/ knowing no fear that our species waz somehow incorrect. & we
are now plagued with rapists & clitorectomies. we pay for being born
girls/ but we owe no one anything/ not our labia, not our clitoris, not our
lives. we are born girls to live to be women who live our own lives/ to
live our lives. to have/ our lives/ to live. we are born girls/ to live to be
women . . .

(n.l.c. #3 exits thru the walls/ n.l.c. #4 enters, searching for her)

n.l.c. #4
she waited on me on the 7th floor corner flat/ our children
wanderin from room to room        ghosts        ghost children
effie        althea        rosalie/ diphtheria deserted blonde
colored girls/ bright-migrant children never runnin
carolinian hills/ never utterin gullah accents/ slurrin words
like bajans/ mountain folk/ they wandered

rosalie        althea        effie/ in white lace dresses
starched for the wake/ celebrated births on 52nd street
swallowed/ like placenta/ when there is/ nothin else
when you rear yr young in dark closets/ like a stray cat
she waited on me by the door/ opened to auntie's room
from my side of the family/ uncles from charleston/
a loyal bartender/ &/ children in bodies
only hintin of ochre soil/ she lingered by the corrupted window

by the fire escape/ soot-sprinkled plants laughed at her
meticulous ventures/ washin sills/ diapers/ my carpenter's
trousers. her hair/ languid in the nape of her neck
a thick wad of soft nap/ above the mole/ she wanted a bob
a fashionable diversion/ to save pushin thick braids off
her chest while she leaned/ over steamin laundry/ the baby
the father/ & the graves. she waited on me at the kitchen
table/ heaped with buttered rice n okra/ heaped with linen napkins
from the allendale wedding/ the children in bodies gorged
themselves on halves of biscuits/ they prided themselves
for lovin me/ the father/ & they waited. & she drew sketches
of her mother/ who had died/ her sisters/ who had died
her father who had died in jacksonville & left her to speak
too proper for a workman/ too poor/ for somethin better
& i waz solid/ waz handsome/ waz kind & delivered her north
delivered her too many to suckle/ & still sass me.
she waited/ her hair so heavy/ her head hung down to fondle
the baby/ warm the baby/ move the baby from colored manhattan
take the baby north to freedom/ to the bronx/ she waited for
deliverance/ for me to return/ from tendin the fire/
from passin for irish/ from the bar where faster women rolled/
from the garveyites sneerin at pale niggahs all livin together
in special wings of tenements/ she waited & she mumbled . . .

(n.l.c. #5 enters. he is the surviving son of the man speaking)

n.l.c. #5
she poured grease over turnip greens/ asked the haitian roomer
to move/ for workin voodoo on the baby/ dyin/ from scarlet fever
warm the baby/ pray/ save the child. he loved his own.
he loved his own. she sweat & brought breath to his blood.
& he lied in the world/ looked over his shoulder/ every step/
to see the burnin cross/ feathers/ ruins of farms/ his father's
tools. she waited by the bed/ fingerin his tuskegee photo/
the carpenter's shop/ the colored pioneers.
the baby waz purple/ foamin at the mouth/ she waited for christ
to reveal himself/ she sang/ compulsively/ to soothe the baby/
ease his entry/ the door never opened

n.l.c. #4
i lay in the cellar/ fractured/ crumbled/ over uneven casing
i crawled without my body/ thru sicilian ashes/
jewish cadavers moanin in the beams/ i crawled to my children

137/

rosalie        althea        effie in white lace dresses starched
for the wake/ roamin from room to room/ swallowed like placenta
my woman waitin/ receivin the spirits/ carolina screams
branded up country slaves/ i made the journey/ to deliver her
to freedom/ the carpenter/ tendin to his own/ movin north
to the bronx.

(n.l.c. #4 exits)

(n.l.c. #1 and #6 enter with a burst of energy; n.l.c. #5 exits slowly. n.l.c. #1
addresses n.l.c. #6)


n.l.c. #1
shall we go to jonestown or the disco
i cd ware red sequins or a burlap bag
maybe it doesnt matter
paradise is fulla surprises


n.l.c. #6
& the floor of the disco changes colors/
like special species of vipers


n.l.c. #1
no real musicians appear after 2:00 there is no dining out


n.l.c. #6
shout hallelujah/ praise the lord!


n.l.c. #1
but shall i go to jonestown or the disco?
if jesus wont fix it/ the deejay will.
my step is off or on
my arms are sweatin in the spotlights twirlin or the sun


n.l.c. #6
pick those tomatoes/ & join us in prayer!


n.l.c. #1
a tango might excite the crowd
a bolero give us salvation


n.l.c. #1 & #6 (in unison)
freak freak freak


138/

*n.l.c. #1*
maybe i shd really consider the blue silk
every one at the office is looking for me on tv
tonite/ if i win i might die/ jesus help me
the kingdom comes


*n.l.c. #6*
god moves in mysterious ways & koolaid is all we cd handle


*n.l.c. #1*
even my aunt promised not to miss us
our children will be so proud/ gd dancers are gd lovers/
but shall i go to jonestown or the disco?
good lovers get married/ god shares the covenant
of marriage/ & marriage is the dance of life/ oh
we get so happy/ we so happy it's sin & we might die


*n.l.c. #1 & #6 (in unison)*
thank-you jesus


*n.l.c. #1*
god loves bringing wealth from the wilderness


*n.l.c. #6*
yes lord


*n.l.c. #1*
at the disco we shout the praises of the almighty
i wrap my arms around you til the end


*n.l.c. #6*
are you ready/ are you ready to/ freak


*n.l.c. #1*
we came here to feel good


*n.l.c. #6*
thank-you jesus


*n.l.c. #1*
to give joy & form to the world

*n.l.c. #6*
thank-you jesus

*n.l.c. #1*
we came here/ yes lord
in our desire/ in hairshirts & satin
yes/ oh to praise the power & the glory
amylnitrate makes you wanna die/ or dance yrself to death
amylnitrate makes you wanna die/ or dance yrself to death
why go to jonestown/ amen/ i say why go to jonestown

*n/l/c/ #6*
yes lord/ i'ma go to the disco/ where i cd dance myself to death

*n.l.c. #1 & #6 (own rhythms)*
shout hallelujah/ praise the lord
shout hallelujah/ praise the lord
shout hallelujah/ praise the lord
shout hallelujah/ praise the lord.

*(n.l.c. #1 dances off)*

*n.l.c. #6*
elegance in the extreme/ gives style to the hours
of coaxing warmth/ outta no where.
elegant hoodlums/ elegant intellectuals/ elegant ornithologists
elegant botanists/ but elegance in the extreme helps most
the stranger who hesitates to give what there is
for fear of unleashing madness
(which is sometimes uninvolved in contemporary morés/
archetypal realities or graciousness). elegant cab drivers.
elegant derelicts/ elegant surgeons/ elegant trash.
elegant priests/ elegant dieticians/ elegant nymphomaniacs/
elegant discos/ elegant shoes/ elegant elevator operators/
elegnt salesmen/ elegant negroes . . . elegant/ elegant/ elegant!
in the absence of extreme elegance/ madness can set right in
like a burnin gauloise on japanese silk. though highly cultured/
even the silk must ask how to burn up discreetly.
elegance. elegance. elegance.

*(n.l.c.'s enter & freeze, as layla begins offstage)*

*layla (o.s.)*
i want to say these things to you/ mostly cuz yr not here.
if you were here we wd kiss/ rub all denim thru . . .
i speak to you a lot/ when i'm alone. i want to tell you
i cannot stop smoking kools/ forget the militia in panama
all brown & bald in gestapo boots . . .

*(music begins as layla enters, surrounded by her night-life companions)*

paradise has her own ugliness: the man on the boat
from dusseldorf/ chasing me to dance with a "colored"/
the first in his life/ this my april in the north atlantic.
at dusk the sea is sultry/ we are not her lovers & she treats
us so.
did you know i have so many secrets i believe are yrs/
what of me? i need you to have & still cant imagine
you ever thot i wanted you to see the posters in rio/
guerilleros' faces taped to steel/ remind me of our struggle.
we merge in our eccentricity/ this penchant for the right to live.
peter tosh awready said: "everybody's talkin abt peace, i
talkin abt justice"/ our kiss is desperate/ long awaited/
known immediately/ unequivocal & not enuf.
tupac amaruo knew what to do. i imagine you in guadalajara
on the back of a donkey/ the 3-yr-old pickpocket will seduce you.
this is not the first time i've swallowed bad white wine/
i've been betrayed by escalators before/ no one knows
you've planted here/ no one knows you find wine tricklin
from my body/ our champagne still squirts from my braids/
even now i am not empty . . . such things i wd say/ tho cecil taylor
long ago passed quevy station/ in the cemetery there
i smelled myself in soil/ bitter & french/ dark & falling apart
in my hand . . . i wd say to you/ a marimba might civilize me/
a fashion fair in bangkok suffocate my sense of style.
jessica swears the yng men in manila dance well/ but
have no minds. i want to hold you in this/ so you might know
what i bring you/ my mouth is full & broad/ my tongue
cluttered with syllables & desire/ even this has not come out
straight/ so many days uprooted/ each time i fly i know again
memory & desire are relentless/ when yr not here to talk to
i speak my most precious/ lay out the mystery/ the devastation/
my honor/ i cant even catch yr eye/ so i trace the skies
with/ these hidden things/ ces choses perdues/
that you might find me/ in the night/ when i am flying.

i want to tell you i cannot stop smoking kools/ forget
the militia in panama/ all brown & bald in gestapo boots/
dontcha wanna be music/ & ease into the fog
dontcha wanna be like rain/ a cosmic event/ like sound . . .

*(layla's night-life companions come alive & join her in the chant/ then slowly*
*disappear thru the walls as layla goes back to sleep/ but the chant is heard as the*
*lights fade)*